A Little Band of Disciples

The Beginnings of Churches of Christ in Madison County, Alabama

John Chisholm Church History Series

C. Wayne Kilpatrick

A Litle Band of Disciples: The Beginnings of Churches of Christ in Madison County, Alabama

Copyright © 2024 by C. Wayne Kilpatrick

Manufactured in the United States

Cataloging-in-Publication Data

Kilpatrick, C. Wayne (Charlie Wayne), 1943–

A little band of disciples: The beginnings of Churches of Christ in Madison County, Alabama / by C. Wayne Kilpatrick

John Chisholm Church History series

p. cm.

Includes name index.

ISBN: 978-1-956811-75-9 (hdbk); 978-1-956811-76-6 (ebook)

1. Churches of Christ—History—Alabama—Madison County. 2. Churches of Christ—History—Alabama—Tennessee Valley counties. 3. Churches of Christ—History—Alabama—19th century. I. Author. II. Title. III. Series.

286.676197 DDC20

Library of Congress Control Number: 2024947440

Cover design by Brittany Vander Maas and Brad McKinnon

Heritage Christian University Press
PO Box HCU
3625 Helton Drive
Florence, Alabama 35630

www.hcu.edu/publications
All rights reserved.

No part of this book may be reproduced in any form or by any electronic or mechanical means, including information storage and retrieval systems, without written permission from the author, except for the use of brief quotations in a book review.

Contents

Foreword	v
Preface	xi
Introduction	xiii
1. MADISON COUNTY	1
2. MERIDIANVILLE	3
3. OTHER WORKS AROUND MERIDIANVILLE	10
4. NEW MARKET	13
5. HUNTSVILLE, TRIANA, AND OTHER EARLY WORKS	18
6. CIVIL WAR AND THE CHURCHES	26
Post-Civil War Conditions of the Church	28
7. JORDAN'S COVE	30
8. MADISON	35
9. HUNTSVILLE	43
10. NEW HOPE	92
11. UNION GROVE	100
12. MADISON CROSS ROADS	104
13. OWEN'S CROSS ROADS	109
14. EAST HUNTSVILLE	116
15. WEST HUNTSVILLE	123
16. MERRIMACK MILLS—HUNTSVILLE PARK	132
17. BEREA—GOOCH LANE	141
ENDNOTES	145
Bibliography	155
Name Index	157
Also by C. Wayne Kilpatrick	160
Heritage Christian University Press	162

Foreword

Sunday lunch in the home of Kelby and Martha Smith was where the Harps were first impressed upon by Wayne and Brenda Kilpatrick. After four and a half years in the mission field of New Zealand, my young family made its way to Florence, Alabama, in the winter of 1985-86 to attend International Bible College (now Heritage Christian University). Wayne was to be one of my professors. His expertise is in the fields of history and the Bible. That spring semester, it was my privilege to sit in his World History II class. With every passing day, it was apparent that Wayne's passion was all things historical. On the first day, he said, "We must always stop and pay respects to the bridges we have crossed." And, for the next thirteen weeks, he filled the air with the stories of the past. To Wayne, it was not just information on a page that needed to be shared; it was not just the former things that needed retelling. To him, and ultimately to those of us at his feet, it was our past, our story—our history. Whether talking about John Tetzel's sales of indulgences to build Leo X's St. Peter's Cathedral in Rome, Italy, or the rise of Oliver Cromwell's Parliamentarians in the defeat of Charles I of England, we were led through a maze of factual details that resonated and gave more profound meaning to our lives.

Charlie Wayne Kilpatrick was born on Possum Creek, near Center Hill, Lauderdale County, Alabama, on December 30, 1943. He became a Christian under the preaching of Alden Hendrix, being baptized by him in 1957. After two years of undergraduate studies at the University of North Alabama, Wayne was drafted into the U.S. Air Force. Before his international assignment, he took the opportunity to continue his education by taking courses at the University of Maryland. At the height of the Vietnam War, it was not long before he was stationed in England's R.A.F. Welford in Berkshire, where he was assigned the task of ammunition inspector. During his term of service, he attained the level of sergeant. Being a history lover in an old country like England afforded him a goldmine of antiquity to examine firsthand. Whenever leave was extended, he was either playing his banjo somewhere in a show with some of his friends or striking out on his own in a planned direction to investigate Britain's ancient culture.

Returning to the U.S. after his term of service, Wayne was employed for 18 months by the Tennessee Valley Authority. He married the former Brenda Elaine Chaney of Leighton, Alabama, on December 12, 1970. At the encouragement of his brother-in-law, Milton Chaney, a gospel preacher, Wayne entered the first class of International Bible College (now Heritage Christian University) in the spring of 1972. He was part of the college's first class since transitioning from the older Southeastern Institute of the Bible. After graduating with his Bachelor's Degree in Bible in 1974, Wayne determined to return to England as a missionary. Working primarily with the Wembley church of Christ in Middlesex, just northeast of London, he and Brenda evangelized in that region. Due to a lack of sufficient support, after a year, the family returned to the Shoals area.

In the fall of 1975, upon his return to the United States, Wayne accepted an offer to teach World History, Bible Geography, and Church History at International Bible College (now Heritage

Christian University). In addition, he enrolled at Harding University Graduate School of Religion (now Harding School of Theology) to study under noted church historian Earl Irvin West. Wayne completed his studies at Harding with a Master of Arts in Religion (M.A.R.). Over subsequent years, he completed twelve post-graduate hours at the University of Alabama and six graduate hours at the University of North Alabama.

The summer following my first class in World History, it was my pleasure to travel with Wayne Kilpatrick to Newport, Wales, UK, where he directed an evangelistic campaign. For a week in the summer of 1986, we knocked on doors, conducted Bible studies in the city during the day, and worshipped with our Welsh brethren in the evenings. One afternoon, we took a break and went about five miles out of town to Caerleon, an ancient Roman city. We walked through the excavated ruins of the amphitheater and the military barracks. A few days following the campaign, we traveled to London, where we had the pleasure of having our own tour guide, C. Wayne Kilpatrick. Whether at the tower of London, Stonehenge, the cathedrals of Winchester, Canterbury, and Salisbury, and just about everywhere in between, the sheer volume of information that seemed to spill freely from this man's mind was nothing short of phenomenal.

Then, there were Kilpatrick's Church History and Restoration History courses. The names, dates, and stories of the past flowed in graceful order from his lips as if he were walking down memory lane. Wayne had a little yellow box with 4x6 index cards that he used to teach his classes. This coveted container of notes was a veritable treasure trove of knowledge he had collected and shared over the years.

Professor Kilpatrick's classes were a magnet to students. His kind-hearted and sanguine spirit filled every lecture with meaningful material that could be used in our ministry for a lifetime. Once, while teaching the history of the Restoration Movement, we arrived at class, and he told us to go to our cars and follow him a few miles from the school. He took us over to Chisholm Highway to a little shanty of a house. We followed him to the backyard, where among a few trees was the small Chisholm Cemetery. Wayne had just been lecturing about how Benjamin Lynn came to Madison County, Alabama, as early as 1809 to establish New Testament Christianity there. He had explained that Lynn's daughters had married men with that pioneer spirit, Rachel to Marshall De'Spain and Esther to John Chisholm, Jr. Lynn died in 1814 and was buried somewhere north of present-day Huntsville. After 1816, the family moved into what is now Lauderdale County, the Chisholms to Cypress Creek, north of Florence, and the DeSpains to Waterloo.

As we approached the cemetery, there before our eyes were the graves of John and Esther Chisholm. John's father, John Chisholm, Sr., was also buried there. He had been an agent for Cherokee Indian Chief Doublehead and rented land on his reserve. More importantly, these people were the first New Testament Christians in Lauderdale County, planting a New Testament church on Cypress Creek. Also buried in the cemetery was Dorinda Chisholm Hall, the young wife of Benjamin Franklin Hall, the Christian preacher who came to the region in the fall of 1826, preaching baptism for the remission of sins. Under his influence came the baptisms of Tolbert Fanning, Allen Kendrick, and others at the hands of James E. Matthews.

History is a science. With this visit to Chisholm Cemetery, pure science—the ideals, the concepts, the people, the facts on a page—became applied science—seeing, touching, experiencing. Pure history became applied history! It was a hands-on examination of the evidence of history. Later that semester, other trips were made, such as to Red River Meeting House in Logan County, Kentucky, where the Second Great Awakening in America's religious history began under the preaching of Presbyterian James McGready in 1799. We also made our way up to Cane Ridge Meeting House in Bourbon County, Kentucky, where the Kentucky Revival reached a crescendo in August 1801. From there, Wayne took us to Bethany, West Virginia, where we witnessed the artifacts, the home, the buildings of Bethany College, and the old mansion that attests to the lives and influences of Thomas and Alexander Campbell. The lectures, the trips, the discussions, and the demeanor made Wayne Kilpatrick the master of his profession.

C. Wayne Kilpatrick is known for his research and journalism. The sheer volume of hours he has spent in front of microfilm and microfiche readers, computer screens, and books in his hands is uncountable. During one Christmas break many years ago, Wayne read the 40 volumes of Alexander Campbell's *Millennial Harbinger*. He has one of the largest book collections of any historian, above 40,000 volumes. He was a staff writer for *The Alabama Restoration Journal*, and his numerous articles appear in many history-related magazines. He has lectured on church history for many churches of Christ, at numerous universities, and other education-based programs across America.

C. Wayne Kilpatrick is an evangelist and successful gospel preacher. He has conducted semi-annual evangelism campaigns through Heritage Christian University in many of the states of the United States and other countries. For 20+ years, he traveled annually to teach Bible and church history short courses in the Yucatan, Mexico.

After assisting the History Department at Heritage Christian University for 48 years, he received emeritus status in 2022. At the end of this year, he plans to retire from his position to focus on researching and writing on Alabama restoration history.

This tome is a testimony to the tenacity and pure devotion of the man. After reading it, this writer has been impressed by the voluminous sources gleaned to make this work possible. I fully commend C. Wayne Kilpatrick for this book, as it will be most appreciated by researchers of the future when they attempt to dig where he dug. It will be a much-prized resource of Restoration History in North Alabama for generations to come.

Scott Harp
TheRestorationMovement.com
May 17, 2024

Preface

For many years there has been a great need for a comprehensive history of the development of the Restoration Movement in Alabama, and the Tennessee River Valley in general. F. D. Srygley's *Larimore And His Boys* was the earliest attempt to capture any semblance of early Lauderdale County Restoration History, although it was only a partial to the whole of this study. Interest began to manifest itself in the early 1900s. In 1903 A. R. Moore presented a historical review to the Alabama State Board of Missionary Society. This was the first work of its kind, but it was written for the Disciples of Christ—keep in mind that the Disciples were still connected to our movement until 1906. This review was never published. In 1906 J. Waller Henry wrote "Sketches of Pioneer Times" for the *Alabama Christian*—a Disciple paper. Richard L. James and Donald A. Nunnelly wrote graduate theses on the Alabama Restoration Movement. In 1965 George and Mildred Watson published *History of the Christian Churches in the Alabama Area*. All of the above-mentioned material dealt with the Disciples of Christ part of the Restoration Movement. It was not until the 1940s that Asa M. Plyler began traveling over the state and collecting material on the early and then present-day Churches of Christ. He covered every county in the state. His manuscript was finally published upon the request of his family. The book was titled *Historical Sketches of the Churches of Christ in Alabama* and no date of publication was given. Plyler's book gave us some "personally collected information; but beyond that, it has not been of much help, as most of his sources were very limited. Today these sources are more readily available, and we have taken advantage of them.

It was needful—yes even imperative that lives of devotion to the Lord's Kingdom, such as the men and women in this study be told. Younger generations need to know what they have. They need to know that these precious servants of the Lord sacrificed so much so we could be where we are today in the Churches of Christ. A generation, now in danger of squandering away the church, needs to appreciate the fact that many of these subjects went without proper clothing, or proper medical attention many times, were constantly in need of financial means, and made many other sacrifices in order to establish the Lord's work in so many places. It would be the greatest act of ungratefulness toward the generations of these preaching brethren, who gave so much sacrificial devotion to helping save the lost and dying world if their story remains in obscurity. We truly are standing on the shoulders of giants, and these—our predecessors were the giants.

We have undertaken the task of producing a history that uses only documented sources—such as church records, journal articles, unpublished autobiographies, documented papers written for schools and universities, published and unpublished interviews, courthouse records, and even monuments and cemeteries. We have limited this study to the four Alabama counties north of the Tennessee River. That is where the Alabama Restoration Movement began.

This book is written to be used, hopefully, as a resource tool to encourage further research into local church histories. Perhaps, the lives of these forefathers in the Lord's work may inspire us to do great things for our Lord and Savior Jesus Christ.

Introduction

The four counties that lie on the north bank of the Tennessee River—Madison, Jackson, Lauderdale, and Limestone—will be the subject under consideration for this work. We will treat the counties chronologically in the order in which the Restoration Movement began.

At first, Alabama was part of the Mississippi Territory, which was ceded by Georgia and South Carolina to the United States. The Territory of Mississippi was an organized incorporated territory of the United States that existed from April 7, 1798, until December 10, 1817, when the western half of the territory was admitted to the Union as the State of Mississippi and the eastern half became the Alabama Territory until its admittance to the Union as the State of Alabama on December 14, 1819.

Prior to the War of 1812, many settlers came into what is now Madison and Jackson Counties, Alabama. Alabama was then still part of the Mississippi Territory. They could not legally, nor safely travel any further into what is presently known as Northwest Alabama because the Indians controlled the land until 1816. Some of these pioneers settled in northeastern Jackson County near modern day Bridgeport, Alabama. another group settled 10 miles north of Huntsville, Alabama, and established Meridianville.

In the years that followed the close of the War of 1812, an influx of thousands of settlers came into the northern part of Alabama from Tennessee, North and South Carolina, Georgia, and Virginia. This was due to the promise of bounty lands to be given to men who had fought in the War of 1812. With each new settler came his own peculiar religious views, resulting in the founding of churches to propagate their views. Along with these settlers from the older states came the views of Barton Stone, James O'Kelly, and a few years later, Alexander Campbell. Just as with other religious groups, the followers of Stone, O'Kelly, and Campbell founded congregations of believers, who were dedicated to spreading the message of the Restoration Movement. Many of these congregations would prosper for a few years and then gradually disappear. Some, however, would weather the storms of time and exist down to the present.

In Northeast Alabama, the Bridgeport (Rocky Springs) and Meridianville pioneers were neither of the James O'Kelley, Barton Warren Stone nor Alexander Campbell groups. These pioneers began their New Testament churches independent of the other movements. Rocky Springs congregation was established in 1811 or 1812 by members of the Old Philadelphia church in Warren County, Tennessee, which had been established by a people who came from a mixture of religious beliefs and who wanted to follow the New Testament pattern They had established their congregation near Viola, Tennessee in 1808. The Gains and Price families moved shortly afterward to Rocky Springs (1811 or 1812). The Meridianville work was begun by Benjamin Lynn in 1808 or 1809. Both groups had studied themselves out of denominationalism without the influence of any of the three above-mentioned movements.

In Northwest Alabama, one such congregation (Stoney Point —established in 1816) has managed to endure. Several other congregations in this area that were established before the Civil

War, were not so durable. Many of them have faded into obscurity.

Much has been written about the political history of this area, but very little has been written about the religious history. Hardly anything has been written concerning the Restoration Movement in North Alabama. F. D. Srygley's biography of T. B. Larimore, *Larimore and His Boys,* sheds some light upon the history of this area and George and Mildred Watson's *History of the Christian Churches in the Alabama Area* gives some insight into this part of the state. Several histories of local congregations have appeared, but many times these works are weighted down by local traditions, rather than historical facts. Due to the lack of knowledge on the part of the average church member concerning the Restoration Movement, the purpose of this study is to give a historical account of the North Alabama movement. Our method shall be to discover who established these works and what caused them to grow or die, whichever the case may be. Since every historical work must have a beginning and an end, we have set the date of our study to begin with 1808–1809, the approximate time Benjamin Lynn came to Madison County, Alabama, and ending with the year 1914, the year World War I began. This time span covers a little over a hundred years of Alabama restoration history. It should be remembered, however, that this is in no way a complete history because there are examples of churches, such as Liberty, which appeared in *The Christian Register* of 1848 as being in Lauderdale County, Alabama, having eighty-five members, and possessing their own house of worship, then disappearing from all written records. Such incidents make it impossible to compile a complete history. History, however, does not dwell upon that which has been lost, but rather that which can be found. This historical study shall be based only on what can be found.

To prepare such historical undertaking many sources have been consulted. Local newspapers of the period under discussion, local courthouse records, journals of historical societies, unpublished histories, and biographical sketches have been valuable sources of material. Many books have been written by our brethren on subjects not related to the Alabama area, yet touching upon it, and literature by other religious groups have proven helpful. There are several historical collections of the brotherhood that have supplied valuable aid in this investigation, but the chief source of material has been found in brotherhood journals beginning with Campbell's first issue of *The Christian Baptist* in 1823, through most major journals until the year 2000. Where occasion has demanded and opportunity has afforded, different portions of North Alabama have been visited and much valuable information has been gained by private conversation. Such were the sources from whence this history is derived. It is hoped that this uncovering of information will give a better understanding of the Churches of Christ in North Alabama.

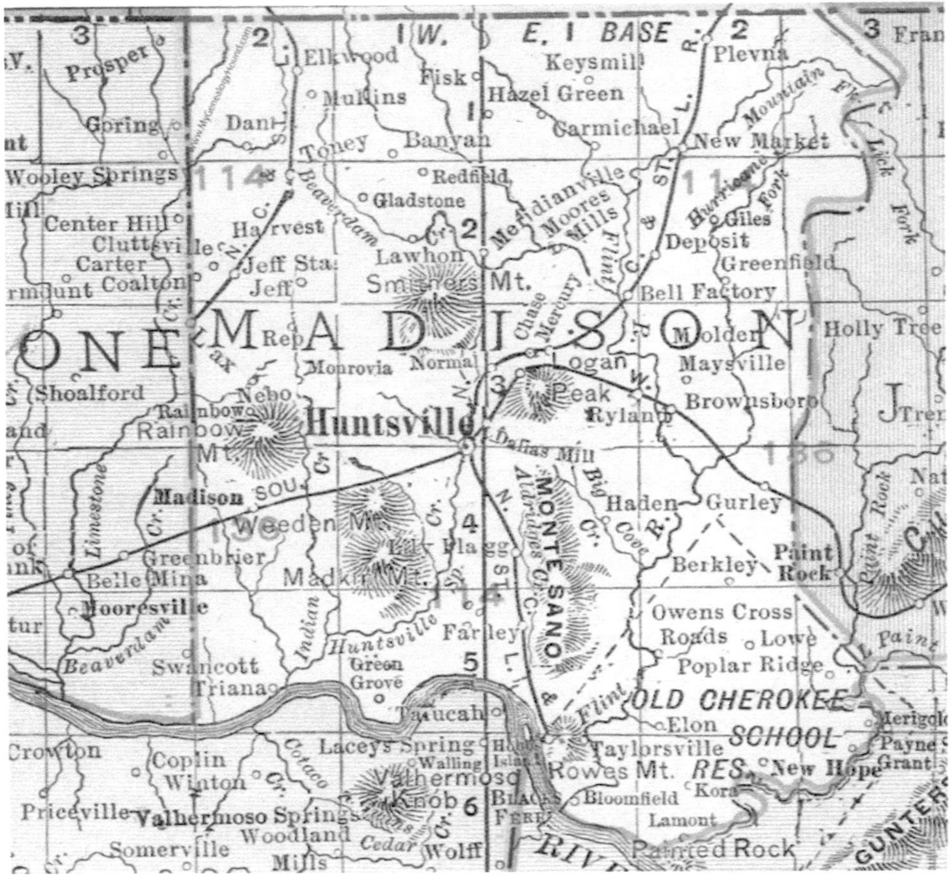

MADISON
Huntsville
MONTE SANO
OLD CHEROKEE SCHOOL RES.
E. I BASE
Plevna
Keysmill
Fisk
Hazel Green
Carmichael
New Market
Elkwood
Mullins
Toney
Banyan
Redfield
Gladstone
Harvest
Lawhon
Meridianville
Moores Mills
Deposit
Giles
Greenfield
Bell Factory
Holly Tree
Maysville
Brownsboro
Logan
Peak
Ryland
Normal
Monrovia
Nebo
Rainbow Mt.
Madison
Weeden Mt.
Madkin Mt.
Flagg
Dallas Mill
Haden
Gurley
Berkley
Paint Rock
Owens Cross Roads
Lowe
Poplar Ridge
Elon
Taylorsville
Rowes Mt.
New Hope
Kora
Bloomfield
Lamont
Painted Rock
Farley
Green Grove
Triana
Swancott
Greenbrier
Belle Mina
Mooresville
Wooley Springs
Center Hill
Cluttsville
Carter
Coalton
Jeff Sta.
Jeff
Prosper
Goring
Shoalford
Laceys Spring
Walling
Valhermoso Knob
Valhermoso Springs
Woodland
Somerville
Mills
Wolff
Coplin
Winton
Priceville
Crowton
Limestone
Beaverdam
Indian
Flint
Cotaco
Cedar
Aldridges Cr.
Big Cove Cr.
Lick Fork
Mountain Fk.
Hurricane Fork
RIVER
GUNTERS

Madison County

Madison County was created by Mississippi Territory Governor Robert Williams on December 13, 1808. Other lands were added until the county achieved its current form in 1824. The county was named for James Madison, who was then serving as secretary of state under President Thomas Jefferson. The county is in the north-central part of the state, bounded to the north by the State of Tennessee and to the south by the Tennessee River. It encompasses 806 square miles. The first white settlers entered the area around Ditto Landing in the south and the area around New Market in the northeast between 1802 and 1804. These early settlers got word back to their former friends and neighbors of the unusual fertility of the soil, the beauty of the country, and of the wonderful "Big Spring," and in 1806, large numbers of homeseekers began to come into the county from Middle and East Tennessee, and Georgia. These pioneers were of the types usually found on unsettled frontiers, "the advance guard of civilization," known as "squatters." They were a very thrifty lot, and at the government land sales, which began on August 9, 1809, many people were able to buy the tracts upon which they had "squatted" and made their homes. They were mostly honest, law-abiding people, and modest in their desires and customs, living peaceably without law or government for some years.

Between the years 1805 to 1809 wealthy and cultured slave owners came into the county in large numbers from North Carolina, Georgia, and Virginia. Soon this class outnumbered the pioneers; these later settlers bought large tracts of land at sales in 1809. The area was previously inhabited by Cherokee and Chickasaw Indians. The first sale of public lands was held on August 9, 1809. Upon coming into the county, the settlers from North Carolina and Virginia moved along the then-western border of civilized customs and cultivated lands into West Georgia and Middle Tennessee, till they reached the Tennessee River, which they crossed near the Georgia line.

Meridianville

Religion followed these brave pioneers into Madison County, Mississippi Territory. Among the earliest pioneer families, was the John and Esther Chisholm family. They originally came from Larue County, Kentucky, near Hodgenville, Kentucky, and settled near Meridianville, Madison County, Mississippi Territory (now Alabama). Esther was Benjamin Lynn's daughter. Lynn was the first minister among churches of Christ to move into Alabama. He and his wife Hannah, and daughter Rachael Lynn D'Spain's family moved next to the Chisholm family. Rachael's husband, Marshall D'Spain, was also a part-time minister of the gospel. Along with the Chisholms, Lynns, and D'Spains came the Matthews, the Crisps, and a host of other families with membership in the Christian Church, also known as the Church of Christ. Some of the Matthews and Crisps families arrived by 1807–1808, as their names appear in the January Tax Records of 1809. Since Marshall D. Spain, Benjamin Lynn, and John Chisholm are not on the January 1809 census, but John Chisholm is recorded as buying land on September 18, 1809, in Huntsville, Madison County Mississippi Territory[1]; Lynn and Chisholm arrived in Alabama sometime in 1809. The D'Spains arrived a few months later, according to another preacher who came into the territory about the same time to spy out the land. That was Abner Hill, who left a diary. He recorded:

> I went with Brother Marshal D. Spain to look at North Alabama and concluded to remove there. I quit riding the circuit, made arrangements and removed to North Alabama when it was a new unsettled country. [2]

Hill gives the year as 1810.

Lynn began meeting with the Christians who had come from Green, Hardin, and Larue Counties of Kentucky to that area of Madison County. Their first meeting place was their cabins and during mild weather, they met under brush-arbors. By early 1814 Lynn's congregation had built a church building. "On Dec 23, 1814, Ben Lynn died at the home of his daughter, Mrs. John Chisholm in Madison County, Alabama near Huntsville and is buried in the Christian Church burial ground there."[3]

From Robert Matthews' family came a son who later became an excellent evangelist. Terry Cowan, co-author of *A Matthews History* 259; wrote of James:

> James Evans Matthews, the oldest child of Robert and Elizabeth Matthews [born on 19 Mar 1799 in Laurens County, South Carolina], distinguished himself as a minister, attorney, and statesman. He was a leading figure in a frontier religious reformation whose adherents were first known as the "Christians in the West." Churches of Christ, Christian Churches and Disciples of Christ evolved from the movement. In later years, Matthews also became well-known in Mississippi political circles.[4]

James E. Matthews spent his early years in Laurens County, South Carolina. In 1811, the family joined other family members in Madison County, Mississippi Territory (now Alabama). James was 12 years old at the time. It was here in the newly erected church building at Meridianville that he became a Christian. His Uncle Joseph Matthews was first located there in 1807, along with other family members and later, some Kentucky neighbors—the Chisholms, Lynns, D'Spains, and Crisps. Together they formed the nucleus of the Church of Christ in Meridianville, Madison County, Mississippi Territory (what is now Alabama).

During the summer of 1814, another preacher came from Kentucky into Madison County to spy out the land. His name was John (Racoon) Smith. He was, at the time, a Baptist minister. [He is mentioned here because he was later converted and became one of the great evangelists in the churches of Christ.] His intentions were to buy land and resell it for profit. He returned to Kentucky settled his affairs in that state and prepared his family for travel to Madison County, Mississippi Territory. He reached his destination in the Hickory Flats, northeast of Huntsville, on November 2, 1814, about seven weeks before Benjamin Lynn died. Hickory Flat was part of the area around Plevna and only four miles north of New Market, Madison County, and about 21 miles from Huntsville.

Smith found an unoccupied cabin, which he rented till he could build on his own land. He began to scout the land in the country around with the intention of selecting some of the best sections of the public domain. August Williams—Smith's biographer—wrote:

> A few Baptists had already moved into the country, some of whom were his father's old friends, from East Tennessee; but they lived some fifteen or twenty miles distant. They heard, however, that a son of George Smith had come into the State, and that he was a preacher of their own faith and order. They sent him a request, therefore, to visit them, and to preach to them, expressing, at the same time, the tenderest regard for the memory of his father. Anxious to know those who already loved him for his father's sake, he accepted their invitation, and left

home, commending with strong faith his family to God, who had so often cared for them while he was away.[5]

On Saturday, January 7, 1815, he saddled his horse, mounted it, and rode to see his father's old acquaintances. Williams further wrote:

> He reached his destination in the evening and was received by his father's friends as a son. Little incidents of family history, the progress of events, the prospects of the country, and especially of the Church, were all talked over at the fireside till a late hour at night, and he retired to rest with a heart full of pleasant memories and still more pleasant hopes.[6]

Meanwhile, back home his wife had been called that evening to the bedside of a sick neighbor that lived near their home. They had sent and begged her to come and cheer the dying woman with her singing; for she had a beautiful voice, and sang with emotion. She heeded the call. John August Williams described the tragic evening as follows:

> She had taken her infant in her arms and gone at twilight on her mission of love. She had left her cabin and the three older children in the care of her brother, and of a younger sister, who also was with them. They had all gone to bed early; for they were tired of the toil, or of the sports of the day. About ten o'clock, while the mother was trying to soothe her afflicted neighbor with her songs, screams of anguish reached her ears, and the blaze of her burning house suddenly lighted up the woods. She seized her baby and rushed to the spot, for the distance was not great. The house, which was built of light poplar logs, was already wrapt in fire. Without, in the glare of the flames, stood her brother, holding one little, trembling child by the hand.[7]

The fire had, somehow, been caught among the rafters of the

cabin. The fire's heat had wakened Hiram Townsend, but it was too late to save the children. Hiram was Anna Townsend Smith's brother, who along with a sister, lived with the Smiths. He hardly escaped with his life. His sister, also awakened by the fire, had rushed through the flames and pulled with her the little girl, with whom she had been sleeping. They could save nothing from the cabin, including two young children. All the family's clothing, their furniture, and every dollar of their money was gone. Heartbroken Anna could not be comforted.[8]

Two men were at once sent to the house where John was lodging and relayed the sad news to John. They brought him his horse, and he hastily began the sad journey home, to weep with Anna. Upon arrival home, he saw Anna in a deep state of grief and neighbors gathering the charred bones of his dead children. Anna soon became ill and died of grief and John eventually traveled the path of grief but was rescued from death by caring neighbors. When he recovered, he went back to Kentucky and a few years later was converted and became a great force in the Restoration Movement. He would make other trips to Madison County, Alabama. His last trip was a sad one. In the late summer of 1843, he returned to Alabama to preach among friends—he now being a minister among the churches of Christ he preached in various communities. One of these locations was Huntsville but with no visible results. He remained among the people of Madison County until November 15, 1843—the day the Campbell-Rice debate began in Lexington, Kentucky. His visit to Alabama, on that day, came to an abrupt sad end. Messengers from Kentucky brought news of his youngest son's death back home. His son fell into a pot of scalding water while neighbors were killing hogs for the Smith family.[9]

In his thesis, "The Disciples of Christ in Alabama, 1860–1910," Donald Alfred Nunnelly says:

> As sad as was "Raccoon" John's experience in Alabama, it may have been what set him on his way to becoming a great force in

Disciple history. He had for many years been a consistent Baptist, but because of the death of his wife and children, he became greatly troubled over the doctrine of election and foreordination and finally joined the independent movement. There he invited people "to stand on the Bible and the Bible alone." He thus became one of the early exponents of union and along with Campbell and Stone led in the formation of the communion of Disciples of Christ.[10]

By the end of 1816, the Cherokee and Chickasaw holdings in Lauderdale County had been relinquished to the U.S. government and were put up for sale and settlement. The Chisholm and D'Spain families, along with others, had left the Meridianville community. This had a significant impact on the congregation at Meridianville. It seemed to fade into oblivion. By 1825 the gospel meetings were being held north of Meridianville and not in Meridianville.[11]

Various efforts were made to keep a congregation in Meridianville, but all efforts seemed to be futile. J. W. Shepherd held a meeting at Meridianville in November 1884. T. C. Little of Fayetteville, Tennessee reported the following:

> Bro. Shepherd is conducting a meeting at Meridianville, Ala., with a prospect for good. The brethren in that section are laboring earnestly for the cause.[12]

An effort in 1946 was attempted and reported by C.C. Burns:

> I am now in a tent meeting on the Huntsville-Fayetteville (Tenn.) Highway, near Meridianville, Ala. We have been running for more than a week. The first night of the meeting we had a tent packed. It was difficult to find another seat. Since the beginning, interest has been growing. It is our purpose to establish a congregation in this community. In fact, the congregation has begun. We had an afternoon service last Lord's day, and several

in the community engaged in all the acts of New Testament worship. Pray for the success of the Lord's work in this community.[13]

Burns' effort was short-lived. By 1964 a group of churches in the Huntsville area re-established the church at Meridianville as can be seen in the following report:

Marvin F. Bryant, 4116 Narrow Lane Road, Montgomery, Ala., 36111, April 22: "In a meeting with the Meridianville church in Huntsville, Ala., April 10-17 there were four baptisms and four restorations. The Meridianville church is about two years old with a membership of 100. Tommy Rosenblum is their preacher."[14]

This congregation is a thriving working congregation in 2024.

Other Works Around Meridianville

Other works were established for brief periods of time throughout the northern parts of the county. In the fall of 1824 B. F. Hall had just finished a meeting in what is now Marshall County, Tennessee at a place called Globe Creek [now called Wilson Hill.] He decided to come down to North Alabama and hold meetings. He held at least two in Madison County, as mentioned by Hall in his unpublished autobiography:

> After the Globe creek meeting, I went further south to attend some camp meetings in North Alabama: one in Gandies' cove, in Morgan County; another in Honeycomb valley, and another at McNutty town in Madison County. As my resources were about exhausted and my clothes well worn; and as I had received but little if any remuneration for my labors; I taught a three-months school in the winter and occupied my leisure time studying medicine.[15]

Hall related an incident that well describes the persecution and the power of God's gospel as good conquers evil:

An incident occurred in Alabama, which I will relate here. I, at a meeting above Meridianville, delivered a discourse on the design of baptism and invited persons to confess the Lord. One young lady came forward, and desired to be immersed forthwith. Her mother was dead. Her father had been a Baptist preacher but had become an apostate and a wicked man. As we were yet talking about the best place to immense in a stream nearby, the old man came up to me, and shaking a large hickory cane in my face, told me I must not baptize his daughter. I inquired: "Why not?" He answered huffishly: "That is none of your business; but"—shaking his cane again at me, his eyes looking daggers—"you had better not attempt to baptize her"—and his large frame shook with rage. Turning to the young lady, who sat weeping, I asked her if she still desired to be baptized? She said she did. "Then I will baptize you at all hazards." I said, and, turning to the audience, designated the place where we would administer the rite. The old man, turning to his daughter, said: "If you are baptized, you shall never enter my house again while you live." The poor girl, looking up at me through her tears, said: "I want to be baptized." An old brother Griffin, a man well to do in the world, who stood nearby, walked up to the agonized girl, and said: "My daughter, you shall have a home at my house." We repaired to the water, and I baptized her, the old man offering no resistance. The young lady got into mister Griffin's carriage and went home with her. A few days afterwards, her father sent for her to return home. She sent him word she would not go then; but if he would bring a horse, with a saddle the next Friday, and take her down to a meeting to be held at McNuttytown, she would go home with him after the close of the meeting.

Accordingly, on the day designated the old gentleman rode up to brother Griffin's, leading a horse with a lady's saddle. The young lady was soon in the saddle, and she and her father were on their way to the meeting.

The next day I preached and gave the usual invitation to

penitent believers to confess the Lord. The old gentleman who was sitting directly in front of the stand, arose instantly and came forward weeping, holding the same big cane in his hand. His daughter sprang to her feet, and uttering an exclamation of joy, rushed forward, and threw her arms around her father's neck and sunk down upon her knees by his side! It was a touching scene to see the father and his motherless daughter clasped in each other's arms weeping—the one shedding tears of bitter grief and penitence; the other tears of joy.

Had not the young lady resolutely obeyed the Lord, brooking the bitter opposition of her wicked father, both would doubtless have gone to perdition together; but now, hand in hand, they were treading the pilgrims pathway to the city and home of God. It is always right for one to do his duty—to obey God. In such cases, all results well.[16]

NEW MARKET

The road from Winchester, Tennessee was a major thoroughfare that entered James Bell's land on his north boundary. It was near that point that a lesser trail diverted from the Winchester Road in an eastward direction for a short distance until it crossed the Old Deposit Road. The trail continued through the hills and divided again. One trail led to the east side of Berry Mountain and the other divided again and threaded its way deeper into Hurricane Valley.[17]

Hurricane Creek begins its course about a mile east of New Market and runs a little south-eastward and its course takes it west of Gurley, Madison County, Alabama. In 1825 Barton W. Stone came and held some meetings in and around the area of New Market. These meetings were publicized in a Huntsville paper. The advertisement read as follows:

> The Rev. Barton W. Stone will preach at Robert Randolph's on Elk River (Ten.) on the 1st sabbath in Oct—next. Wednesday following the 5th at the schoolhouse near the Beaver Pond, (Al.)- Thursday the 6th, in Huntsville-Friday, Saturday, and Sabbath following, he will attend a camp-meeting at Giles McAnutty's, on Hurricane fork of Flint River.[18]

This is the first published notice of Stone having come to Alabama, except for John Nelson Biard's family history which tells of Stone preaching in Limestone County in the 1830s.

In 1827 the same James Matthews who lived near Meridianville [when a boy], wrote a report on camp meetings in North Alabama and South Middle Tennessee as follows:

> Our next Conference will be held at Hurricane, Madison county the first Lord's day in February 1828. I subjoin the names of the preachers belonging to this Conference.
>
> ORDAINED. — Elisha Price, John H. Parkhill, Elisha Randolph, Mansel W. Matthews, John M'Daniel [McDonald], Thacker V. Griffin, Isaac Mulkey, William Clap, Crocket M'Daniel [McDonald], Robert Baits, Jonathan Wallis, James E. Matthews, Reuben Mardis, E. D. Moore.
>
> UNORDAINED. — James Anderson. Lorenzo D. Griffin, Jonathan G. Ward, Wm. J. Price, Mm. W. Wilson, Andrew Russel, Jonathan Parker. [19]

This is the first report ever made in Stone's *Christian Messenger* or Campbell's *Millennial Harbinger*, or any other monthly journal, relating to the work found somewhere on the creek in Hurricane Valley. We do know that in the northern part of the valley, near New Market was a campground for religious purposes. We are not sure what became of this work. Was it just a camp meeting used by religious groups for seasonal gatherings, or was it an established work that failed early? This one report is the only scrap of information available on Hurricane Valley. About fifty years later another work, referred to as Hurricane Grove, was established further down that valley and was located a few miles from present-day Maysville. The work to which Matthews referred was nearer to New Market than Maysville. We believe that the Hurricane camp meetings laid the groundwork for the New Market area churches that followed.

In 1830 a baby boy was born to the Jessie Randolph family near New Market, Alabama. His name was Coleman L. (C. L.) Randolph. He was the first child born in Madison County, Alabama to grow up and become a gospel preacher among churches of Christ. He began preaching in his twenty-first year. He also became a great educator. At the time of his death, he was President of Waters and Walling College in McMinnville, Tennessee. I. N. Jones of McMinnville, Tennessee wrote in Randolph's obituary:

> Bro. Randolph was born near New Market, Madison County, Alabama in 1830 of poor parents, and having lost his father before he was grown, was taught the lesson of self-reliance early. At an early age he began school-teaching, and about 1851 commenced preaching. My impression is that he made his first effort at a discourse at Liberty, Marshall County. As his means would allow, he would attend college, and thus add at intervals to his stock of knowledge. Finally, in 1855 he graduated at Bethany, Va. His ability as a teacher needs no enconium from my hand. His preaching was of that plain, modest, pathetic character peculiar to a man of no ambition for fame nor desire to wound the feelings of opposers.[20]

He may have been the only Madison Countian to graduate from Alexander Campbell's Bethany College. Randolph preached in and around New Market for four or five years before moving to Tennessee. Sometime between his graduation from Bethany College in 1855 and 1859, he moved to Richmond, Lincoln County, Tennessee where he and H. H. Harris established "The Journal Of Education."[21]

Another Randolph —William B. Randolph is found preaching in and around New Market, Alabama in 1845. He was an older brother of C. L. Randolph. Tolbert Fanning [Editor of the *Christian Review*] wrote of W. B. Randolph:

> Bro. W. B. Randolph, of Ala., asks "If a man must forebear preaching when unacquainted with the languages, if his church be unwilling and unable to educate him?" By no means. If a young man can speak English, knows the truth, and possesses other requisite qualifications, he should exert himself to promote the cause of his Master. It is, however, a reproach upon the churches, that they are employing no means scarcely to qualify and sustain young teachers. Bro. Randolph is an estimable young man, as I have the best evidence to believe, and is very desirous to acquire knowledge. Will the brethren in his part of the country enable him to attend some institution which will afford him the requisite facilities'! Why not raise a fund to educate destitute preachers? The managers of Franklin College will subscribe liberally for the education of Bro. R. and others who will give themselves to the ministry of the word. Do the disciples feel no interest on this subject? T. F.[22]

Randolph wrote an article from Newmarket, on September 10, 1845. He devoted his life to preaching in various places throughout Alabama and Tennessee. Later that year Fanning wrote again of Randolph's continuing work:

> By a communication from Bro. John N. Lewis of Louisville [Loweville?], Ala., I learn the Mormons have had, heretofore, considerable influence in that section. A debate was recently held in that region between Bro. W. B. Randolph and a Mormon. and it is confidently believed by the brethren, that one of the vilest isms of the day has received a severe wound. It is the duty of the saints to live down and argue down all systems opposed to Christianity.[23]

Loweville was in Madison County according to an official U.S. Government document.[24] This debate demonstrates the ability Randolph had, even without formal training at that time.

The Madison County Randolphs were just as formidable as the other Alabama Randolph preachers who will be discussed in another chapter.

Huntsville, Triana, and Other Early Works

A very peculiar item was printed in Campbell's *Millennial Harbinger* in April 1834. It was reminiscent of the apostle Paul's reference to the trumpet that gave an uncertain sound, (1 Cor 14:8) in that it gave information; but not enough to aid in locating a congregation or who Daniel Olds was. It creates more questions than answers, as will be seen in the report:

> BROTHER Daniel Olds, of Madison county, Alabama, and the disciples around him, should, in my judgment, meet every Lord's day to keep the ordinances of the Saviour.[25]

This note is the only information we have of Daniel Olds and nothing about where he worshipped or with whom. Was it the remnants of the old Meridianville work or Hurricane or was it the beginning of the work at Triana or some now unknown work in Madison County? It is tantalizing to guess on the where, and the who, or what happened. The only thing that can be deduced from this information is that a Daniel Olds was a member of the church somewhere in Madison County, Alabama, and his brethren were having difficulty understanding the proper times to meet and partake of the Lord's Supper.

William Henry Wharton of Tuscumbia, Alabama gave an insight into the religious conditions in Huntsville in his letter to Walter Scott in 1834. We give the letter in its entirety:

BROTHER SCOTT,

I am a resident of Tuscumbia Alabama; I have an introductory letter to you from Bro. E. A. Smith of Ky. who passed through our place some six weeks since. It was my intention to have called to see you; but as it is a little uncertain whether you have returned from your excursion to Virginia, and I am in great haste to proceed eastward, I have concluded to defer it until my return, five or six weeks hence. Brother Smith was in Huntsville in January and preached some eight or ten times; the weather being exceedingly unfavorable he had but few hearers; he excited a good deal of enquiry as well as much opposition; two or three weeks after he left, I visited that place by the particular request of some of the brethren there and remained a week. I was denied the use of all the meeting houses of the place, but was permitted by the Officers of Justice to occupy the Court house, an old and inconvenient building; having once been a resident of that place and being personally acquainted with most of the citizens, after my first appointment I had quite a respectable audience, which continued to grow in number as long as I remained, and indeed we were compelled to adjourn to some other house; but as no other could be procured, although several of their; Churches' were unoccupied, we were permitted by the kindness of the Thespian Company to occupy the Theatre. I had the pleasure during my absence of introducing two into the kingdom of our Lord. The public mind is at this time much excited upon the subject of this great salvation; at that place as well as at other parts of North Alabama every form of misrepresentation and opposition has been used; but our trust in the living one is, that the veil of prejudice which has been thrown over the minds and hearts of people will be rent in twain, and truth, radiant truth, majestic and sublime, will shine into their hearts and give to dying mortals the light of the knowledge of the glory of God in the face of Jesus the anointed one.

The boat in which I am going on, will stop only a couple of hours and I am in great haste. I did desire greatly to see your face and shake your hands in gratitude to God our Heavenly Father who through the instrumentality of your labors has imparted to me so much favor and mercy, joy and peace in believing the gospel concerning his Son.

I was formerly an elder in the Presbyterian Church and for obeying Peter, into whose hands the keys of the kingdom were given, I have been discarded, called a Campbellite, opposed, calumniated, mis-represented, abused, denied entrance into houses consecrated to the worship of the only living and true God as an authorized teacher of the living Oracles; but although I have been cast down I am not destroyed; though opposed, not overcome; but in the midst of persecution I have enjoyed more of the blessedness of believing, more of the comforts of the Holy Spirit, peace of conscience and joy of heart than I had ever hoped to attain to in this life.[26]

Note the persecution of Wharton because he left the Presbyterian Church. The sectarians were like the Jews who followed and persecuted Paul. They were relentless. Wharton seemed to bear up under the persecution with a strong faith in his Savior. By October he had established the church in Tuscumbia, as will be discussed in another book.

Racoon John Smith returned to Madison County in the fall of 1834 and gave a sad picture of the spiritual conditions of this part of Alabama. He wrote in a letter dated August 22, 1834:

Bro. J. T. Johnson, a few days since, I returned home from a tour of 32 days length. In which time I passed through several counties in this State as far down as Wayne, and Cumberland. Thence through 6 or 7 counties in Tennessee. Thence into Madison co. Alabama. I can now assure you that the Christians in this section of the country, see but a small corner of the field, which loudly, loudly calls for laborers.[27]

From what was written by Wharton and Smith one can see that the spiritual conditions in Madison County were dismal in the 1830s, but things were on the brink of looking up in this area of Alabama.

In 1844 Fanning came to Huntsville. He gave the following account:

> Tuesday, the 12th, I travelled thirty miles to Huntsville, in Madison county, Ala., and finding my appointment had not preceded me, I slept free from the cares and anxieties of life. I remained during the 13th and preached at night in the Baptist meeting house, to two ladies and six gentlemen, and a few colored [sic] people round tho doors, and I think it was one of my happiest efforts. Huntsville is a beautiful town, with a population of about 2000 persons, who are intelligent and no doubt excellent people with reference to worldly matters; but most of them are prejudiced against the Christian religion. The professors are under the influence of imaginary revelations, and where this is the case, the Bible is little respected. There are a few noble friends of the truth, and I trust the time is not far distant when the day star will dawn on this village. At present, the people are, through the influence of their preachers, afraid of the truth. Bros. Caldwell, Putnam, and Malone should hold up the light to their acquaintances.[28]

Other places in the county were now beginning to hear the gospel preached. Triana was a work that had been planted by 1838 or 1839. We know nothing about who started that congregation, but we find a clue to the earliest time in that place. In an obituary of John Conoley printed in the *Gospel Advocate* of January 26, 1882, it was recorded:

> Died, December 29th, 1881, at his residence in Mooresville, Limestone county, Ala., our venerable brother, John Conoley. Bro. Conoley was born in Essex county, Va., in the month of February 1779, thus being at the time of his death nearly eighty-three years of age. He moved from Virginia to the State of Alabama in 1836. In 1839 he became a member of the church of Christ, joining the congregation of disciples at that time meeting in the town of Triana. Thus, it will be seen that, for more than forty years, this noble old soldier of the cross has steadily fought under the banner of King Emmanuel; and it is the verdict of all who knew him, that he made a good fight ....[29]

By 1843 the village of Triana was gleaning much attention as is shown in a letter sent to Tolbert Fanning:

> Bro. D. G. Ligon, of Moulton Ala., who was immersed in June 1843, has zealously advocated the cause of his Master, at all convenient seasons, ever since, and writes, that "on a visit to Triana, Ala., seven most intelligent persons became obedient to the faith." Prospects are also good for many other additions.[30]

Later that year another report came forth from Triana by G. W. Elley:

> Triana, 15 miles S. of Huntsville, Ala., June 20th, 1844. Messrs. Editor: I have by accident attended a meeting here of some days, with Bro. D. G. Ligon a part of the time, which has resulted in 13 valuable additions, and the removal of much prejudice on the part of many, although our teaching has greatly excited some of the religious people as usual. Contrary to all my expectations when I left Columbus, Miss., on the first of this month. I have been compelled from a sense of duty to yield to the calls of the brethren here to remain in this beautiful valley some 7 or 8 weeks, to aid the cause of the Bible and truth. The Lord willing, I shall endeavor to scatter the good word of truth as fast and as

thick as possible. When I leave, I desire to visit Murfreesborough, Lebanon, Hartsville, Gallatin, &c. in Tennessee. Yours truly, Geo. W. Elley.[31]

Elley followed the above report with another report on the whole valley on the north side of the Tennessee River in September 1844:

> To the Editors of the *Christian Review*: Messrs. EDITORS: I have just closed a second meeting at this place, with 20 more additions —making 33 added to the church in Triana, since my stay in this region. At other places there have been gained 8 — making 41. Among the above number, there were 4 Methodists, 1 Baptist,1 Episcopalian, and 1 Cumberland Presbyterian. I also had the pleasure of congregating 13 brethren and sisters at Somerville, in Morgan county, with fair prospects of doing good. —I am grateful to my heavenly father for the acquaintances which it has been good pleasure. to make in Triana, Morrisville [Mooresville], and Somerville, and generally in North Alabama. I have never met with a more hospitable and interesting people; and their attention and kindness shown to us and especially to my afflicted wife, while· our sojourning among them, will long be remembered with gratitude. In the above number, there are many who are among the choice spirits of the land.
>
> The whole valley of North Alabama, from Huntsville to Florence, is a delightful country, highly cultivated, and filled. up with a population of much intelligence and moral worth. With one or two exceptions, I have found people everywhere anxious to hear our teaching; and I must specially invite. the attention of our teaching brethren to that part of Alabama. I have never seen a more interesting field for doing good, and the cause we plead demands that special attention be given to that region. The few brethren and sisters we found at Triana acted their part with great devotion to the cause. I was also greatly aided and refreshed

by the continual company of Bro. N. Hackworth, who conducted all the singing-truly an important work. —In a day or two I leave for Kentucky. Yours truly, Geo. W. Elly, Triana, North Alabama, Aug. 6, 1844.[32]

Even though Elley mentioned Somerville (in Morgan County) and Mooresville (in Limestone County) which are discussed in other chapters, he gave a particularly good account of the Triana work. Thus, it appears that Triana must have been established sometime in late 1838 or early 1839. Within five years the congregation had grown to fifty members or more.

Fanning made a visit to Triana later that year. He wrote in his *Christian Review*:

> Sat. 14th, I travelled some fifteen miles to Triana, a pleasant little village in Madison county, and found a very excellent congregation of disciples of Christ. At this place I preached day and night till Tuesday, the 17th; and although, the beloved brothers and sisters were much encouraged and strengthened, there were but two additions. Notwithstanding that most of the members are young in the cause, they are generally intelligent, and I trust they will grow fast "in grace and the knowledge of the truth." Bro. J. J. Ward is a young man of promise, and I hope he will direct his talents and energy to the Lord's honor.[33]

During this period David Ligon preached periodically for the brethren at Trian as the following report reveals:

> Three people have been added to the Lord recently at Triana and Mooresville, Ala., by the labors of Brother David G. Ligon. May the Lord bless the disciples in that section of country. T.F.[34]

In November of 1845 G. W. Elley made plans to come back to Madison County, as is seen in his report:

On the 8th inst. brethren J. T. Johnson, W. Morton, and myself, expect to leave home for the Huntsville region of North Ala, on a preaching tour, and we trust in the Lord for the success of the truth. May the Lord help us! G. W. Elley.[35]

With the success of Elley and Ligon in the last several months, at Triana no doubt he would return there to visit and preach to the brethren. Remember the brethren at Triana had been extremely kind when Elley's wife became extremely ill during his preaching at Triana over a year before.

A disturbing fact became clear in December of 1848 when Alexander Hall published his *Christian Register*. The *Christian Register* gave a list of churches in each state by county. Madison County had no congregations listed. Was there no practical work in the county by 1848 or were there no leading men who had the initiative to report to Hall? We do know that truly little relating to the work in Madison County from 1845 until after the Civil War has been recorded. What happened? Maybe that can be discovered someday.

George and Mildred Watson do not treat the history of Madison County in their book, until 1947, when the first Disciple church was established.[36] In his work on Alabama, Asa Plyler leaves a gap with no information on Madison County, spanning 1840 to 1880.[37] One can see there was a void of information concerning the Madison County work from the 1840s until the 1870s, and then the information was scarce.

Civil War and the Churches

No pen can accurately describe the chaotic conditions that prevailed in North Alabama just after the close of the Civil War. Alabama had only been admitted into the Union in 1819 and was hardly out of the pioneer stage when war came in 1861. The demoralization brought on by invading armies, the derangement of the labor system by the sudden emancipation of the slaves, the depression sustained in their loss as property, and the shock of disappointment at the failure of the Southern arms—all these conspired to produce deep and universal gloom. For once, society was launched upon a wild and stormy sea of disorder. Men and women wept in the midst of crushed hopes. Soon the weather-beaten Confederate soldiers began to return to their homes to find prevailing the wildest disorder. But the Confederate brought with him the same spirit, which had carried him through hundreds of battles. He exchanged the battlefield for a field of cotton or corn. This was a period of distress and gloom, which was not relieved by the events of the immediate future, as we shall later see.

The country along the Tennessee River was hotly contested ground during the Civil War. The river, in connection with the Mississippi, opened direct steam-boat transportation to the base of supplies for whichever army held possession of it. By holding the Tennessee, the Confederate Army could reach the rich agricultural regions of west Tennessee, Arkansas, Mississippi, and Louisiana, and communicate with such important supply centers as Paducah, Memphis, and New Orleans. With this same facility the Federal Army, if in possession of the river, could reach Paducah, St. Louis, and all ports along the Ohio River. For this reason, the Tennessee Valley was one of the great battlegrounds of the Civil War, second only to the Shenandoah Valley of Virginia. Each army managed to own the transporting supplies and munitions of war over it. The armies moved back and forth across the river so that the country was almost constantly a battleground.

Union and Confederate soldiers used church and school buildings for hospitals and quarters for themselves and even their horses. When the Union troops occupied these buildings, they destroyed them internally and many times burned them to the ground, so the enemy could not use them.

In Madison County there is no direct account of any of our brethren having a building that was treated in such a way; but if they even had their own meeting places, they most certainly would have suffered the same fate.

In Huntsville, all that was left of the original First Methodist Church building just off the square on Randolph Avenue, was a silver chalice charred from the fire accidentally started in that church's basement during January 1864 while occupied by Union Soldiers.

We also give examples of some surrounding communities to show how the entire valley suffered the same conditions during the war. Union forces moved into the First Presbyterian Church in Athens. They chopped up the pews for firewood, eventually gutting the building, including chopping out floor joists, leaving a shell. The same thing happened to the church building belonging to our brethren at Salem, Tennessee about 17 ½ miles northeast of New Market, Madison County, Alabama. All that was left was the pulpit and the shell of the building, making it unusable. The building built to replace the old one still stands. These malicious acts were repeated time and time throughout the South, especially in North Alabama.

This great period of gloom was felt greatly by the Churches of Christ in this county, also. These churches had just gone through the most traumatic period of their history. The task of trying to tell how our brethren functioned as the Lord's body during these dark and bloody years, now seems almost impossible. These were the silent years of the Restoration Movement, concerning history. The religious historian is left to pick his way and gather up the fragments of history as best he may.

Post-Civil War Conditions of the Church

F. D. Srygley quotes T. W. Caskey, who served as a Confederate Chaplain during the war, concerning the aftermath of the war:

> When the war closed, the South was a land of desolation and ruin. There was scarcely a home in all the country that did not mourn the loss of its own dead. In many homes the absent dead outnumbered the desolate living, and in every case the loved, but lost, were the strength and support of the family. It was a land of disconsolate widows and helpless orphans. Every heart was burdened with sorrow and every home was shrouded in gloom. There was no place in all the South but had its evidence of the ruin of war and ravages of famine. With such evidence continually before every eye, no heart could for a moment forget its sorrow.
>
> If the people came to the house of God for the comforts of religion, they probably found the walls of the church pierced by shot and the floor of the very sanctuary itself stained with the blood of their beloved dead. If not so bad as that, they at least found the ashes of campfires about the church, or the deep ruts of wagon trains along the road. There was scarcely a horse or a mule in the whole country that did not have the familiar army

brand, and the people were compelled to clothe themselves in garments made from cast-off and worn-out army uniforms. It was difficult to find a man in the whole country who had not either lost a limb or received a wound in the army.[38]

The first ten years were almost unbearable, because of the Reconstruction laws, which to the southerners was like no law. These laws were imposed upon the South and were used by northern opportunists to make themselves wealthy at the expense of the poor Southerners. Drought followed on the heels of the war making the southerners almost helpless. Evangelism suffered greatly during this period and records were almost nonexistent.

The first mention relating to the church after the Civil War was not so good. It seems that a man posing as a minister among churches of Christ was a scammer. The secular papers published charges against a man called Webb. The report was as follows:

> The secular papers are publishing some grave charges against one I. I. Webb of Madison Co., Ala., who has been representing himself to be a Christian preacher but who, if guilty of the charges preferred, should be shunned by all respectable people. He is said to reside near New Market.[39]

We do not know what became of the man or the charges made against him. Nothing else was mentioned concerning him through the pages of the *Gospel Advocate* and it said nothing of the work in any of the churches in the county—just the warning concerning Webb's fraud. This incident does help illustrate just how vulnerable our brethren were after the war.

Jordan's Cove

The first report made after the war, concerning evangelism in Madison County, was made by Robert Wallace (R.W.) Officer, who had recently left the Baptist Church. This report came to the *Gospel Advocate* near the end of the year 1879:

> Brethren L. & K: On the fourth Lord's day in October, we had one addition with the congregation at Verona. From there I went to Tullahoma, Tenn. Our M. E. friends (Northern) opened their doors, and I talked to the people there on Thursday night; on Friday night at Salem; the brethren are alive there. First Lord's day in November one added to the congregation in Jordan's Cove. Monday morning at 8 o'clock, Bro. George Lester married, and left at 11 o'clock for Ohio with his young wife, a worthy sister. On Tuesday following, Dr. Macon and Wm. McCrary and wife were buried with the Lord in baptism. They are the first in their settlement in the reformation; they have a nice frame house, built by their own energies; there is a good work begun there, between New Market and Huntsville, Ala. The brethren there would be glad for any of the talking brethren to call and give them a lesson. Will Bros. George Faris and G. Lipscomb please give them a call?

I am now at Bunker Hill. Bro. Dixon buried a promising young man with the Lord this morning at this place and left for home. I will remain a few days. R.W. Officer Bunker Hill, Nov. 10, 1879.[40]

A new congregation was named for the first time. It was Jordan's Cove near Maysville, Madison County. It appeared suddenly and disappeared just as quickly. New Market and Huntsville were mentioned also but nothing said of a congregation in either location. This area running from near New Market down through Maysville was known as the name Ryland/Maysville/Brownsborough area. (Jacque Reeves, editor, *The Huntsville Historical Review*, published by the Huntsville-Madison County Historical Society, 2008, 128).

The work done in this area may have been the forerunner to the Maysville work which came many years later.

Another early glimpse of the church in Madison County after the Civil War was given in 1880 in the *Gospel Advocate*. Brother R. W. Officer writes:

> The meeting at Oakland, Madison county, Ala., closed last Thursday night—ten additions. A congregation of thirteen covenanted to keep house for the Lord. May God bless the happy little band. Bro. G. A. Faris was with us and did some good preaching.[41]

Oakland was a favored place to preach for Officer perhaps because he had organized the congregation. He made other visits to Oakland even after he moved to Texas later that year. The congregation was still worshipping at Oakland in 1884. J. W. Shepherd was conducting a school near the church, according to sister Winnie Wilson of Scott's Station, Kentucky. She had sent $5.00 to aid Shepherd's work. He had been preaching at Huntsville and other places in that section. She wished him abundant success.[42] Thus, we know the work at Oakland was still functioning as an organized church in 1884. Later this congregation was lost to time and now no longer exists.

About a year later another report on the Madison County work is made by a brother at Maysville. He was William F. Jordan Jr. Dr. Jordan was living in that community on June 1, 1860.[43] He wrote to the *Gospel Advocate* on August 29, 1881, concerning the labors of a brother John Marcrom (of Decherd, Franklin County, Tenn.,) It told the following:

> I have the pleasure of reporting through your valuable paper a part of labors of Bro. John Marcrom, this spring and summer. At his regular monthly appointment Lynchburg, Tenn., had one addition, and at the County Line, Tenn., embracing 2nd Lord's day in August had seven additions by baptism. He began a meeting in Jordan's Cove near Maysville, Madison county, Ala. Saturday before the 3rd Lord's day in August and continued until the Friday night following was assisted by Bro. J. H. Morris of New Hope, Madison county, Ala. The gospel of Christ was ably presented, to the people, and am happy to say that twenty-three gave heed to their preaching, twenty made the good confession and were baptized, two restored, one from the Baptists. Others seemed almost persuaded to become Christians, but the love for the world was the strongest. A short time ago a controversy arose with our brethren in regard to extending the right hand of fellowship to young converts. Some said it was not taught in the Bible and was now practiced by a good many congregations. We would like very much to hear from you on the subject; we do not want to do anything contrary to the teachings of God's word.[44]

Dr. William F. Jordan became a prominent member of the Jordan's Cove work. His family had a very good influence on the work at that place.

Robert Wallace Officer came on the 5th Sunday of July 1882.

It seems he was raising funds for his mission work as he had moved to Texas at the end of 1880. It was reported in the *Gospel Advocate* that Officer would preach at two locations in Madison County during July—Oakland and Jordan's Cove:

> Bro R. Wallace Officer will be at Oakland, 4th Lord's day in July; Jordan's Cove 5th, all in Madison county, Ala; at Tullahoma 1st in August, Thursday before; Bethel, Wilson county, Tenn., 2nd Lord's day; 4th at Bunker Hill, and at Alexandria, Tenn., commencing Saturday night before 2d Sunday in September next.[45]

This could have possibly been Officer's last time to visit Jordan's Cove. One question is still to be pondered—just when was the Jordan's Cove work established? We know the work had been started by November 20, 1879, as previously reported in the *Gospel Advocate* Just what became of the Jordan's Cove congregation is unclear. It may have morphed into another work, or it may have simply died, like other early works that came and then disappeared across North Alabama.

Another congregation was set up in 1880. J. H. Morris of New Hope, Alabama wrote:

> The fifth Lord's Day in October I preached near Owens X Roads, Madison county, in a new schoolhouse which resulted in the wife of Bro. Mathewson confessing the Lord and being baptized. She for many years was a devoted Methodist. I baptized her husband four years ago; since that. time he has been a devoted and zealous disciple of Christ. He has patiently borne the persecution of his neighbors and malice from the sects. But thank God, prejudice is giving way, and many are almost persuaded to be Christians. If any of the preaching brethren pass that way, please stop and preach for them, they will be well cared for.[46]

Now we have the approximate date of the beginning of Owens Crossroads church.

Madison

1880 had been a good year for the Madison County work. T. B. Larimore was invited to preach in the town of Madison as was recorded by F.D. Srygley in *Larimore and His Boys*:

> The same year (1880) he was requested by a Presbyterian lady to preach in the little town of Madison, Madison County, Alabama. Brothers Herrin and Elam, two of his pupils, accompanied him to Madison, as did his wife. We had a few members there; but no effort had ever been made to establish a church, nor had any of our brethren ever preached there. The meeting resulted in several additions to the church, and steps were immediately taken to build a house. In a few months we had a good house and a good church there.[47]

First, we note that at once after the church was organized the congregation began efforts to secure property and build a church building. One of the earlier ones was from W. A. Odeneal, Pulaski, Tennessee. It was for one dollar, which was close to the amount that most people could afford at that period in our history.[48]

By the time Srygley had written his book in 1889, almost nine years had passed. The church had quite a struggle in getting a building erected and the cost paid. The brethren had to ask for donations far and near to get the project finished. The effort would not be easy; however, the contributions began coming into Madison. The effort did move slowly as the following reports will show.

The first mention of a building in the *Gospel Advocate* was a simple report on money sent to help with construction costs: it was stated as follows: "Another dollar in our care for church at Madison, Ala., from W. A. Odeneal, Pulaski, Tenn."[49] This was one of the earliest responses for aiding the work at Madison, apart from support by individuals connected with the church at that place.

The next response reported:

> Six dollars more have been sent for the church in Madison, Ala., since last week's report. Let the good work go on. Send to this office, or to Mrs. W. S. Patterson, Madison, Ala.[50]

Another dollar was sent to the *Gospel Advocate* for the church at Madison.[51] L. H. Wilson had been sent by the church in Scott's Station, Kentucky. As is shown in the following report:

> L. H. Wilson, of Scott's Station, Ky., returned home last week from Alabama, where he had been sent with money for the Madison church. He reports the prospects bright for a new house and a large membership.[52]

Support kept coming to aid the building project at Madison. Sister McMullen reported receipts from various places in May:

> Sister McMullen reports the receipt of the following for the Madison church: Miss Lucie Wilson, Chestnut Grove, Ky., $5.00; W.D. Vincent, same place, $1.00; Thos. Davis, Youngstown, Ohio, $5.00.[53]

It was announced in the fall that the church building at Madison, Alabama, would be ready for occupation by the last of September.[54] By December T. B. Larimore came and spoke in the new building. The following description of the building was given:

> Bro. T. B. Larimore preached today, Nov. 12, in our new house at Madison; one took membership, Sister Blackwell. The house is a little beauty. We owe nearly $500 on it; have another coat of plastering to put on, then kalsomine; have no chandeliers or lamps as yet. S. J. Kennerly, of Gainsville, Texas, sent two dollars last week; please report through the Advocate. Bro. Srygley will preach next Lord's Day at Madison. Bro. Dr. L. H. Wilson is with us. Bro. J. A. Harding, of Winchester, Ky., will be here on the last of this month. We are anxious to get our house paid for. —A. F. McMullen, Huntsville, Ala., Nov. 12, 1882.[55]

By the end of November, Harding arrived at Madison and began his meeting. He gave his readers a quick view of his meeting:

> The meeting at Madison Station, Alabama, is still progressing. We have received 11 additions up to this present writing, (Dec. 12th,) four of whom came up last night. The interest has been steadily growing from the beginning to the present time. Bro. Leonard Dougherty, of Kentucky, who is with me, adds very much to our success by the excellent way in which he conducts singing. At the close of this meeting, we expect to go to Valdosta, Georgia. J.A. Harding.[56]

Even with men like Larimore and Harding preaching on occasions, the young congregation still had questions arise that they did not know how to settle among themselves. They always depended on the editors of the *Gospel Advocate*, and especially

Lipscomb, for reliable answers. The two examples that we give will suffice to illustrate their growing pains at Madison.

First, Harding's meeting had ended sometime in early December and by January. L. H. Wilson, whose name comes forward as one of the leading figures in the congregation at Madison, was asking advice on a serious question:

> Bro. Lipscomb: What do you think the Scriptures require a church to do in regard to members that have moved away without taking letters and have not added themselves to any other church? Please answer through the Advocate. In Christ your brother, L. H. Wilson. Madison Station, Ala., December 26, 1882.[57]

The answer came back that letters were misused and never used to dismiss members from a congregation but to commend them to another congregation with whom they might wish to affiliate.

Second, by March, another question had arisen—that of a single individual taking the Lord's Supper, or not taking it. L. H. Wilson wrote again to the *Gospel Advocate*:

> Bro. Lipscomb: Do you believe God requires a Christian male or female to eat of the Lord's Supper upon the first day of every week, whether anybody else does or not? When neglected, do you think it is a sin in the sight of God? Please answer through the Advocate. In Christ your brother, L. H. Wilson. Madison Station, Ala., February 25, 1883.[58]

The answer was a mixed one and very opinionated. Lipscomb's answer to this question can be found in the *Gospel Advocate* of March 15, 1883. These questions were not unique to Madison. They were the kinds of questions that arose in most newly formed congregations and not every one of these could not be addressed when visiting preachers came and labored with these infant churches. Thus, the *Gospel Advocate* became the sounding board for these problems.

In the winter of 1882, James A. Harding was holding a meeting at the time V. M. Metcalfe visited Madison. Metcalfe wrote a report on this visit:

> Bro. J. A. Harding's meeting at Madison, Ala., was a good one. About twenty-five or six were added to the church. I had the pleasure of being with him two Lord's days. He did some good sound gospel preaching that aroused the brethren to greater activity and caused sinners to cry out, "what must I do to be, saved?" It always does one good to meet with a man of such strong faith as Bro. H. He also has with him, young Brother Daugherty, from Hart County, Ky. Bro. D. leads the singing, and does a great deal of other valuable work which is important in a protracted meeting. I have heard many of the best singers in the United State, and I say, without flattery, I have never heard his superior, if his equal, especially for his age. Bro. Harding is certainly very fortunate in getting him to be his companion in the gospel; and the church or community that succeeds in getting them to hold a meeting may expect a joyous, happy time, and improvement in every way. They expect to hold a meeting at Valdosta, Ga., and also at Tuscaloosa, Ala., this winter.
>
> Brethren, these servants of the Most High will not beg nor urge you to give money for their support, but I take the liberty of asking you to be liberal with them, as they are poor and need help. While at Madison I met with Bro. Dr. Wilson, to whom the brethren at Madison are more indebted for a house of worship than anyone else. He lives in Shelby County, Ky. Heard through the Advocate that the brethren at Madison were poor and struggling to build them a house of worship. He left his home and moved among them—went to work—not only gave of his money, but got others to give, and superintended the work, doing a great deal of it himself; and now has the satisfaction of seeing one of the prettiest houses in all that section, and a

large congregation of disciples. He says he cannot preach, yet he wants to do all the good he can while the Lord lets him live in this world. I also had the pleasure of meeting Sister McMullen, of Huntsville, who went to Franklin College many years ago. She is an earnest disciple of Christ. May God bless this noble band of disciples and keep them at work all around them for the Master ....[59]

Apparently, Metcalfe did not say what some of the members at Madison wanted him to say. He was mildly scolded by Bro. O. M. Hundley in the following article:

Dear Bro. Lipscomb: In the Advocate of January 18th, I have read with interest the articles, "Notes of Travel," by Bro. V. M. Metcalfe, in which he writes lengthily about our new meeting house at Madison; namely, "While at Madison I met with Bro. Dr. Wilson, to whom the brethren at Madison are more indebted for a house of worship than anyone else." Also, that he "superintended the work, doing a great deal of it himself; and now has the satisfaction of seeing one of the prettiest houses in all that section, and a large congregation of disciples." I regret exceedingly that Bro. Metcalfe has been misinformed in reference to the origin, progress, and completion of our sacred and much beloved house of worship. Complimentary, however, to Bro. Wilson, I will state that he and bis sister have furnished us one hundred dollars towards building the house that cost us nearly nine hundred dollars, including the lot. Bro. Wilson also left his home in Kentucky, came among us, and has done much in his zealous and ardent way in harmonizing and keeping together our little band of brothers and sisters. In a word, we all appreciate him very highly, and regard him as a pure Christian gentleman. But in justice of many of our brothers and sisters who contributed freely, and who labored daily in erecting our little house, I must state that Bro. Wilson was not in Alabama from the commencement to the completion of our meeting house. In conclusion, I sincerely hope that Bro. Metcalfe will find out and report all the co-workers in this little temple of God and render merited honor to whom honor is due. Yours fraternally, O. M. Hundley.[60]

Immediately preceding the Hundley complaint, was Metcalfe's attempt to pacify Hundley. Just why Metcalfe's correction was printed before Hundley's complaint is puzzling. Maybe Lipscomb was letting Metcalfe's explanation appear to have been intended to be corrected before they received Hundley's letter. Metcalfe's correction is as follows:

> In my last notes I gave a short account of Bro. Harding's meeting at Madison, Ala., also of the building of the meetinghouse at that place. I should have mentioned several others who were liberal and active in building the house, among them a good sister who now lives at Mooresville, (do not remember her name), Also Bro. Hundly of Huntsville, God has blessed him with means, and he is using it for his glory. Possibly the house would not have been built for several years yet if it had not been for his liberality. May God bless all his dear children who are working for his glory.[61]

We must observe here relating to brother Orville Marion Hundley; a few years later he and his wife will be a very volatile force in causing the church in Huntsville to split over liberalism—and especially the organ controversy.

The building and Harding's meetings dominated the pages of the *Gospel Advocate* in reporting the Madison work for some time. The debt on the new building was not yet fully paid and a trickling of support continued to come to the church at Madison. A sister Winnie Wilson sent money to multiple works as is shown in the following report:

> Sister Winnie Wilson, of Scott's Station, Ky., sends two dollars and fifty cents to church at Madison Station, Ala., two dollars and one fifty cents to church at Huntsville, Ala., and five dollars to our young Bro. Shepherd, who is conducting a school near Oakland Church, Madison County, Ala., and preaches at Huntsville and other places in that section. We wish him abundant success.[62]

This report references the work at Oakland and the new work at Huntsville. It also mentions that J. W. Shepherd was working in the Madison County Area. By 1889 the work was attracting preachers from as far away as Texas. Elijah Hansbrough, who was from Texas, came to Madison Station July 25, 1889.[63] We assume he preached on Lord's Day, but nothing was mentioned in Hansbrough's article about preaching there.

L. B. Jones held a meeting at Madison in 1907. There was no follow-up report.[64]

The final reference to this work before the end of 1914 was from J. J. Horton who reported from Madison, Alabama, He gave the results of his meeting — "9 days, 4 baptisms. Brother Martin, of West Huntsville, Ala., led the song service. Fine interest throughout."[65] Nothing else appeared in the *Gospel Advocate* or *Firm Foundation* from 1913 until 1915.

Huntsville

The work in Huntsville, according to F. B. Srygley, was apparently pioneered by T. B. Larimore. He wrote:

> About this time (1880), he visited Huntsville, Alabama, and delivered a series of sermons. This was the beginning of a work which resulted in the establishment of a church in that city. In later years, when it was decided to build a house of worship in Huntsville, he took the field and traveled several weeks to raise funds to help complete the house.[66]

Six years later Srygley's reference to Larimore's involvement is substantiated by a report in the *Gospel Advocate*[67] in which Larimore had committed himself to stay the entire month of July 1886, to raise money for the building project in Huntsville church. This will be discussed in more detail later in this section concerning the Huntsville church.

Shortly after the beginning of the church in Huntsville the little band of Christians felt the loss of one of its prominent families' patriarch—John H. Hundley, who had been instrumental in establishing the church at Mooresville in Limestone County. He had served as an elder at Mooresville until sickness compelled him to step down. His life and guidance over his family were strongly felt in the church at Huntsville. His obituary gave the following facts:

> Our beloved and venerable father, Elder John H. Hundley, died at his home, on the evening of January 3rd, 1881, after an illness of several months. Well may it be said of him, "How blest the righteous when he dies." Although we are grieved to give him up, yet it is a sweet consolation to know that he was a veteran soldier of the cross, an earnest and faithful laborer in his Master' a vineyard for thirty years, and now, having completed his eighty-fourth year, he has left us, to dwell in a far better home to meet his just reward, and to give an account of his faithful stewardship. Not only will his sons miss the wise counsel of a kind father, but his faithful wife, herself nearing four-score years, who has stood by his side through life's rugged trials, will miss the sacred companionship of a noble husband. Yes, his neighbors, friends, and especially the poor will ever remember the many deeds of charity and words of comfort he has oft-times extended them in hours of adversity.[68]

The Hundleys became a very prominent family in the Huntsville church. Oscar, Orville's son, became Huntsville city attorney, state representative, and state senator. He lived with his family in Madison in the 1860 census but afterward was counted in Huntsville. Oscar's uncle Orville Hundley would be a factor in the new congregation for nearly fifty years. His family would give the lot on which their first building would be built. The Hundleys were loyal to the ministers who sacrificed so much to establish works in their communities. One of Hundley's favorite preachers was T. B. Larimore. This relationship began when Larimore came and held a meeting at Mooresville, in the last week of June 1877, which resulted in eleven additions to the church.[69]

No doubt Larimore felt partly responsible for the brethren in the city of Huntsville since he laid the groundwork for the establishment of that congregation. This is another case of—Paul planted, Apollos watered, and God gave the increase—Larimore sowed the seed in 1880, Harding came in 1883 and watered the crop of Christians in Huntsville, and God gave the increase.

The next meeting of which we have record was held, beginning in early April 1883, by James A. Harding. A brief note appeared in the *Gospel Advocate* at the beginning of the meeting which read: "Bro. J. A. Harding is now in a meeting at Huntsville Ala."[70] By May the meeting was still in progress.

One anonymous donor sent five dollars for Harding's expenses while he was preaching in Huntsville. This was reported in the *Gospel Advocate* by one of its editors:

> A brother sent five dollars to this office last week for Bro. J.A. Harding, stating that it was a contribution for his labors in Huntsville, Ala., as he understood he went, trusting in God for remuneration for his service.[71]

The meeting was perceived as a success even before it ended. The following report expresses the joy of the little band in Huntsville:

> Bro. Harding's meeting at Huntsville still progresses and the interest increases. Fourteen additions up to May 3rd. The house is packed and jammed every night. Bro. Dougherty aids greatly by his fine singing.[72]

He closed the meeting on June 7, 1883, with eighteen additions that night.[73] Harding either remained in Huntsville for the remainder of the year or came back in the fall or early winter. He held a meeting in the courthouse, sometime, during the winter months of 1883. Someone sent the following report:

> On account of his health, he (James A. Harding) thinks best to spend his winters South, and summers in the North, which he

has been doing for several years. Last winter he held several good meetings in the South, among them one at Huntsville, Ala. A few disciples at this place had been trying for many years to establish the cause of truth; but they were poor and weak. They wrote to several prominent preachers to come and help them. One of them replied, if they would deposit one hundred dollars in the bank to his credit, that he would hold them a two-week's meeting. Bro. Harding, hearing of their struggles, determined to go to their help. He, in connection with his faithful co-laborer, Bro. Daugherty, (the singing brother,) held them a good meeting, resulting in over twenty additions, and establishing the primitive gospel on a firm footing in one of the most important cities of the South.[74]

The language in this report is so much like a later report written by David Lipscomb, that we are led to believe Lipscomb authored this report also. This note was appended to a longer article written by J. W. Shepherd, as appears below.[75]

In July, a sister from Huntsville wrote this note to the *Gospel Advocate*, hoping that the congregation could build a house of worship. It read as follows:

We have seen a letter from a sister in Huntsville, Ala., which says: "We have no preacher, but meet every first day to attend to the Lord's supper. There are thirty-two names enrolled; seventeen of the number meet regularly; have forty-nine dollars in the treasury. We sent Madison church ten dollars today, to help them pay the debt on their house; besides helping some of our needy members. We wish to commence building this year."[76]

Following these meetings, one would think the brethren would have a good meeting place in which to worship—but the struggle continues for this infant congregation.

Between the writing of the July report and October, J.W. Shepherd moved to the Huntsville area to work in the Madison

County churches. He worked in a concerted effort with the little band in Huntsville. In the report, already referred to above, Shepherd mentioned the need for a building in which to meet and worship:

> Dear Brethren and Sisters in Christ: Our little band of disciples has been struggling against, the mighty opposition of poverty and sectarianism for a long while. The opposition is so great at times that it seems to be almost impossible to overcome it at all. What we need now is a comfortable house in which to worship. We have been meeting in the county courthouse for a year and a half, but this is nothing more than a borrowed house. We desire to build a good comfortable house, here in this city; but we cannot, unless our brethren and sisters will heed the Macedonian cry, "Come over and help us." We have a lot and about one thousand dollars subscribed to begin with. The apostle exhorts the disciples to bear one another's burdens" and this burden is too great for us to bear alone. Now we appeal to every congregation of disciples in the United States, to send us one Lord's day's contribution. Hear our cry, dear brethren and help us in this, our time of need. Do not let us sink, when you, by a united effort, can help us so much. Huntsville has between five thousand and seven thousand inhabitants, and is located in North Alabama, on the Memphis and Charleston railroad. Let everyone who reads this appeal make it his duty to bring the matter before the congregation of which he is a member. then it will surely be brought before every congregation. Send remittances by post-office money order or by registered letter, to Capt. O. M. Hundley or J.W. Shepherd, Huntsville, Alabama. Remember, one contribution from, the one Lord's day from the organization of which you are a member will help wonderfully in this grand work. Huntsville, Ala., J.W. Shepherd.[77]

Lipscomb's addendum was as follows:

Huntsville is a thrifty, growing place, and the centre of a good country. But the truth has only lately been planted in the city or country. The brethren are few, are without houses of worship, and the country not well supplied with teachers. The little band in Huntsville is a faithful, devoted band, and has done well to raise what they have. They need help. We believe any church, or any brother, would do a good work to help them. We will gladly receive and forward any amounts sent us for them. D. L.[78]

Harding returned in March of 1885 and co-labored with J. W. Shepherd in a protracted meeting. He wrote:

P. S. Instead of going to Oxford, N. C., as I confidently expected to do, until last Thursday or Friday, I came to this place, Huntsville, Alabama, and am now in a meeting, co-operating with Bro. J. W. Shepherd, of this congregation.

We have just begun, but the prospects are most flattering. Not by any planning of mine, but by the over-ruling of God the change was brought about.

My correspondents can address me here till further notice. The meeting will probably be continued for about a month ... J. A. H.[79]

Harding reported on this meeting and Lipscomb restated it in a follow-up note:

In a note from Bro. Harding, we learn three have confessed the Savior and were baptized the same hour of the night. Interest in meeting unusual and will probably continue several weeks. Bro. Harding wrote under date of March the 3rd.[80]

The next note in the *Gospel Advocate*, just below Lipscomb's statement was a note from sister A. F. McMullen in the Huntsville church. It was as follows:

Sister A. F. McMullen writes from Huntsville, Ala.: "We are having a grand meeting, crowded house. Two confessions tonight and baptized the same hour. Nothing ever like it in Huntsville before. The weather (is) fine. Bro. Cartwright is slowly improving.[81]

The second week of this meeting Harding reported, "There had been seven or eight additions at last reports and good interest."[82] On the third week, he reported, "Seventeen have been added to date. It will probably close on next Lord's day."[83] As of the present time, the final report has not been found—thus we can only speculate as to the overall success of this meeting. We do know that seventeen souls were added to the church in Huntsville. That is a success in any meeting.

As a side note to Harding's coming to Huntsville instead of going to Oxford, North Carolina; a controversy between Harding and J. B. Briney developed. Briney accused Harding of coming to Huntsville, instead of going to North Carolina because more money was involved.[84] If one studies Harding's preaching career they will find many places he preached gave him nothing for his labors. Many times, people who were not from the communities where Harding labored would send him money to aid his work. Briney's charges were not fair to Harding.

The dire need for a building of their own was growing to a critical point. J. W. Shepherd had written that the church was meeting in the courthouse. As early as April 30, 1884, contributions began to trickle in for the Huntsville building fund. Sister Winnie Wilson, of Scott's Station, Kentucky, sent two dollars and fifty cents to the church at Madison Station, Alabama, two dollars and fifty cents to the church at Huntsville, Alabama, and five dollars to young J. W. Shepherd, who was conducting a school near Oakland Church, Madison County, Alabama, and was preaching at Huntsville and other places in that section.[85] The church at Franklin, Tenn., sent $9.50 for the Huntsville, Alabama building fund.[86] The struggle to exist as a congregation had begun and it would be a tough one too. V. M. Metcalfe wrote of the struggle Huntsville Christians in securing a house of worship:

> The little faithful band of disciples at Huntsville, Ala., have for years been laying by them, as they were able, a small amount, and have now enough to buy them a lot on which to build a house and half complete it; they need help to finish it this year. Those godly women, sister McMullen, Collins, as well as Bro. Hundley and his faithful son, (few are blessed with such) and others that I might mention are lending every energy to hold up the standard of the primitive gospel in their midst. They are worthy and need help. Who is not willing to take some small stock?[87]

Sometime in the next few days, a lot on which to build was given to the brethren. The Hundley family, through the encouragement of sister Hundley, accomplished this gracious act. The *Gospel Advocate* reported:

> The congregation at Huntsville, Ala., deserves special mention as a struggling band who have maintained their Christian courage amid difficulties that many would have given up under. They will soon commence building a comfortable house of worship. They have enough money already to build the walls and cover the house. Sister Hundley gave them the lot in a central location and of great value. They have been for several years meeting in private houses, in the courthouse, and at present are meeting in the U. S. Court room, which they can only get for a short time, hence they must either build them a house or go to private houses to meet, which are entirely too small for the congregations at present. They have everything to encourage them. With such women as sisters McMullen and Collins, and a few old brethren as well as rich young brethren as Oscar Hundley, who are willing to take up the cross and bear it

nobly for Christ, they cannot fail. It is a noble little band and deserving of help.[88]

To get the building constructed different men took to the road to raise money for the project. A. C. Henry was one such man. This report was made by one of the editors at the *Gospel Advocate*:

> Bro. Henry is now in Nashville. We hope the brethren will not only make his visit pleasant, but profitable. He certainly is engaged in a noble mission. We should all be willing to help those who try to help themselves. The little band of disciples in Huntsville is doing nobly. Now, brethren, help plant firmly the cause of Christ at this place, make it a radiating center for the gospel. Many of you can give at least ten dollars for this purpose and be infinitely better off. Will you, do it? "To him that knoweth to do good, and doeth it not, to him it is sin."[89]

William Anderson of Carters Creek, Tennessee authored the next report of Henry:

> Bro. W. Anderson, of Carter's Creek, Tenn. writes: "Bro. A. C. Henry was with the church at Beech Grove last Lord's day and at night. Gave us two good discourses on the importance and work of the church. Bro. Henry is travelling in the interest of the little band of disciples at Huntsville, Ala. They need a house and are not able to build. He is soliciting aid of the congregations he visits, for that purpose. We feel sure the brethren can do a good work by responding to the call, as liberally as they can, let it be much or little. Now, brethren, let each congregation do a little to help the cause at Huntsville. We are one body — ought to help all we can. Bro. Henry is worthy; and engaged in good work. We hope the brethren in Tenn. will receive him lovingly and respond liberally."[90]

This effort paid off and money began to trickle into the brethren at Huntsville. By the middle of the summer, things were looking up for the small band of Christians. V. M. Metcalfe paid them a visit and wrote in the *Gospel Advocate* about their struggles:

> The little faithful band of disciples at Huntsville, Ala., have for years been laying by them, as they were able, a small amount, and have now enough to buy them a lot on which to build a house and half complete it; they need help to finish it this year. Those godly women, sister McMullen, Collins, as well as Bro. Hundley and his faithful son, (few are blessed with such) and others that I might mention are lending every energy to hold up the standard of the primitive gospel in their midst. They are worthy and need help. Who is not willing to take some small stock?[91]

Seven days later, Metcalfe wrote another note concerning the church at Huntsville, which was printed in the *Gospel Advocate*:

> The congregation at Huntsville, Ala., deserves special mention as a struggling band who have maintained their Christian courage amid difficulties that many would have given up under. They will soon commence building a comfortable house of worship. They have enough money already to build the walls and cover the house. Sister Hundley gave them the lot in a central location and of great value. They have been for several years meeting in private houses, in the courthouse, and at present are meeting in the U. S. Court room, which they can only get for a short time, hence they must either build them a house or go to private houses to meet, which are entirely too small for the congregations at present. They have everything to encourage them. With such women as sisters McMullen and Collins. and a few old brethren as well as such young brethren as Oscar Hundley, who are willing to take up the cross and bear it

nobly for Christ, they cannot fail. It is a noble little band and deserving of help. V. M. Metcalfe.[92]

Later another letter gave a vivid description of the faith and struggles of this tiny group of a dedicated band of mostly women. Amanda McMullen wrote this letter. She was the main cause for Larimore coming years earlier, and preaching and getting the group gathered. sister McMullen was a woman of "pluck and grit" as J. M. Barnes described her. She wrote:

> Mr. J. M. Barnes: Dear Brother: First, I want to thank you for your kindness and Christian Spirit, in speaking of the needs of Huntsville church. Everyone who reads it here will bless you for it. I have twenty times since reading the piece, wished we had more of such men as "The Little man."
>
> You do not know of our many, many struggles and conflicts: you know something of them. There are four male members who very seldom attend, and there are six-others, who do not attend, and, out of the ten, only two are willing to attend, or, rather, conduct the Lord's day meetings; and it has happened twice that neither of those two were present. But the "Lord will provide," and did provide on each of these occasions. On one of these occasions a brother who lives in Fayetteville, and who has never conducted the service, attended our meeting; and I asked him to conduct the service for us. He said he could not as he had never attended such a thing. I told him it was not too late to begin. After talking to him for a while, he agreed to do the best he could for us, and we had a delightful, sweet meeting, and all went away feeling better.
>
> On last Lord's day there was not a man in the house, save a visiting brother who lives in Morgan county, a Bro. Russell. He went to school several years ago to Bro. Larimore. He is a preacher. He is sound and clear on Bible subjects. Some of our male members were sick, others were absent from town, is the reason they were not at the meeting. There are fifteen sisters

present; we had a nice song service and Sunday school. There are eight widows in our church. There are only two families in our church that do not have to work for their daily bread. Both of those have donated liberally towards the building. Capt. Hundley and wife have given the lot and five hundred dollars. We who are poorer have done all, all we are able to do, for a while at any rate. We are so anxious to build! We cannot do much in the way of building up tho cause until we have a house of our own.

We have been refused every church house we asked for; have used the county courthouse for a long while (eighteen months) and was forbidden the use of it longer; secured the U. S. C. H.; was turned out of that by some mean sneak writing a complaining letter to Washington City. My Irish blood was up to the boiling point, and I sat down and wrote to the Department of Justice at Washington myself. I addressed my letter to A. H. Garland, the attorney-general, and they kindly and nobly gave us permission to use the house. I wish I could tell you in fewer words all that we have had to contend with; someday I hope to. Now, I want you to cheer our preachers once more, by writing to the good Texas brother and telling him we would appreciate and ever feel grateful to him for any amount he would send us. We desire to build a house costing about five thousand dollars. We will have to build a brick, as the lot is so near to the square. The city officials will not permit a frame house within a certain distance of the square. We want our house as central as possible. The lot is the prettiest in town. Bro. Barnes, I know my letter is a blotch, but I could do no better, writing at the store, for I have to stop every few minutes to wait on customers.

Dr. McMullen has been sick nearly three weeks, but he is now able to walk around the room. Several of our little band are sick, and we are so few we miss them when they are absent.

I must close as it is almost time for me to leave the store. Remember us in your prayers. My love to wife and the little ones. May God bless us all as he sees we need and are worthy. Write to me.

Affectionately and Fraternally, Mrs. A. F. McMullen. Huntsville, Ala., May 7th, '86.[93]

Justus McDuffie Barnes was so impressed by sister McMullen's courage and fight he thought her letter worthy of being printed in the *Gospel Advocate*. He wrote a postscript to her letter which began as follows:

> Bros. L.&S.: There are so much pluck and grit in this letter that I would be glad to see it in print. I will state otherwise. There are so much faith and zeal manifested. I wish all of the readers of the Advocate to read and enjoy it, with me. It does one good to now and then to see how noble spirits meet difficulties. After all, only those who fight on and on in the face adverse odds are heroes in the strife. I have handed this letter to the brethren to read. I have read it to my wife, and now I send it to the readers of the Advocate. Now sisters, one and all, drop a tear of joy that you have such struggling band of noble sisters. Take a day, go around, and get up all you can for the Huntsville church. Two sisters at Cross Roads made up money in this way for a nice, silver-plated service for the table, and last Lord's day they were placed on the table, much to their credit. One of the same zealous women mounted a horse, with a companion, a few years ago, when was burned down and my wife and children had no shelter and rode over the country calling upon the brethren and friends to help the man who had preached to her since she was a little girl, and who had taught her years before. She succeeded. See what women can do. What will you do sisters? Please do something, and send the money to sister McMullen, and write me a card that I may rejoice with you and her. Your Brother. J.M. Barnes.[94]

Anyone in any of the Huntsville area churches should be proud of the ladies who, in many cases, led the struggle to see the church established in their communities, by pleading with preachers to come and preach to them. Sister McMullen was one such lady—in fact—she should be at the top of the list. V. M. Metcalfe met her at Madison during one of J. A. Harding's meetings (1882 or 1883) and he was impressed with sister McMullen. He wrote of her:

> I also had the pleasure of meeting Sister McMullen, of Huntsville, who went to Franklin College many years ago. She is an earnest disciple of Christ. May God bless this noble band of disciples and keep them at work all around for the Master. V. M. Metcalfe.[95]

Thank our heavenly Father for such courageous ladies, who desired the gospel to be preached in their communities when most of the men of the day had their minds set upon worldly gain and not spiritual things. Not everyone was proud of sister McMullen's effort to secure a house of worship in downtown Huntsville. A note about a little "misunderstanding" concerning where to build the house of worship was published without a name attached —signed simply "A sister" from Watertown, Tennessee. Obviously, she did not understand all the facts as to why the building was to be located on that particular lot. The letter was judged as harsh toward the church in Huntsville:

> Bro. Barnes: I see in the Gospel Advocate of June 2nd your appeal to the sisters for help for the church at Huntsville. I believe the church there is worthy and ought to receive help. We are too prone to grow selfish in our Christian work. We are ready and willing to help the needy at home, when not willing to aid those farther off. This should not be, for souls arc as dear to God in one place as another. But the question arises, is it right for poor people to give of their hard-earned means — means saved by much self-denial, to build costly church houses, while all around us are precious souls that need the gospel

preached to them, and for the lack of money it is not being done?

Would it not be better, therefore, if the Huntsville church is not able to build so costly a house, that they buy a cheaper lot and build a cheaper house? A very neat and substantial house can be built for one thousand dollars. At least we know of one that cost about that amount.

If it should not be in the central part of the town; if it should not be a fine and fashionable church, or a popular place to go, 1t would be none the worse for that in the sight of God. But it would be a place where the poor, as well as the rich, might feel at home. And would not a faithful, humble, trusting band of disciples in such a house be regarded with more tenderness and love by the meek and lowly Nazarene, than they would be in a fine house purchased with the money that should have carried the gospel to the poor? We should ever remember that the teaching of Jesus was for simplicity of life and character.

No, Bro. Barnes, do not ask us to assist in building fine church houses, but put an evangelist, one that will be loyal to the Lord, in that field in Alabama, which is so destitute of the gospel, and then ask us for help, and I think you will find some sisters so true to God that they will help you all they can in such a work. A Sister. Watertown, Tenn.

We do not understand that the brethren at Huntsville are going to build a fine house for the place. Ed.[96]

The next letter was a response to the letter written from Watertown, Tennessee, on behalf of the church in Huntsville:

> The Huntsville brethren (the earnest ones are nearly all sisters) think the letter of "a sister" published in Advocate two weeks ago, calculated to do them harm. We are sure "a sister" did not intend to injure them, but to benefit them. They state this. They found it difficult to buy a lot. A sister who owned a good lot proposed to give it, if they would build on it. It was a better lot,

better situated than they had hoped to be able to get. The sister was not willing to let it be sold and buy a cheaper one. It is within what is called the "fire limits" of the town. That is the town prohibits wooden houses within the closely built portions of the city. They are therefore compelled to build a brick. They do not think they could build a brick that would be passable for less than the amount called for.

Nothing else could be located on this subject by the Watertown correspondent. The struggle for a meeting house continued. By June 15th Larimore had begun an extended meeting in Huntsville. It continued until June 28th. At this point, brother R. W. Norwood visited for two weeks in Huntsville during Larimore's protracted gospel meeting. He described the situation as he saw it, at the time, in part of a lengthy letter:

> I will give you a few lines, to let you know something of the work done at the places named during the last few weeks; and if you think worthy, you may submit the same to the columns of your most worthy paper.
> On the 15th of May, I landed for the first time, in Huntsville; where I remained two weeks, and enjoyed the interesting meeting with the good brothers and sisters of that place. It is not necessary to say to the readers of the Advocate, that they had good preaching; for, it suffices to say that brother T. B. Larimore, did the preaching; he delivered fifteen discourses; only one accession, and that from the Methodists; yet the good of a meeting is not known by the number of addition only. The brethren there claim a great victory for the truth, and themselves also, very much edified.
> Our brethren there are few, but true and tried. They know no such word as "fail." Brother Larimore has agreed to travel on behalf of the church there to raise money, to help them out in the great undertaking of building a house there, in which the

disciples can worship, and where none dares to hinder; molest or make them afraid.

They are now meeting in the U. S. Courthouse but, dear brethren of Huntsville, be not discouraged, be faithful, for the Lord will fight for his people.

I do hope. and pray that the good brethren, who receive Brother Larimore may chance to go, will open their hearts, and their pocketbooks, and help him to bear his burden. We closed our meeting there, on the 28th... R. W. Norwood, Landersville Ala., June 9th, 1886.[97]

One can see just how difficult a field Huntsville really was and why the congregation remained so small for so many years. When a man like Larimore could baptize only one person after preaching fifteen sermons; the citizens in Huntsville were extremely attached to the "cares of the world."

After finishing his protracted meeting in Huntsville, Larimore promised to stay and raise money for the building project, as has been noted earlier, in this writing. He spent the entire month of July in Huntsville to help raise money for the building.[98] His stay is described in the following report:

> Bro. Larimore is in the city in the interest of the house at Huntsville, Ala. He will spend the month of July at this work. We have heretofore spoken of the just claims of the little band for help. First it is a faithful, earnest and devoted band of disciples. They have done what they were able to do themselves.
>
> Huntsville is a thrifty growing place, the center of a large and growing section of country, in which there are few brethren to aid in building up the cause. We trust then that the brethren will give a cheerful and hearty response. They desire to build this fall and the sooner the help is bestowed the quicker the work will be done.[99]

Help kept trickling into the church at Huntsville from

various brethren and churches. The church at Franklin, Tenn., sent $9.50 for the Huntsville, Alabama building fund.[100] Others sent various amounts for several months to complete the construction of the building.

On June 30th sister McMullen writes again. This time she also sent a letter from California, relating to the funds needed to build a house of worship. Lipscomb published her letter and made closing comments favorable to sister McMullen and the little group of Christians gathered in Huntsville:

> Sister McMullen, of Huntsville, Ala., sends us the following letter from California, for publication. She writes a letter overflowing with gratitude and thanks for the help and friendly expressions and of good will and encouragement in this letter. We think it deserves publication for its sound, scriptural teaching concerning Christ and his love for the humble and poor. We believe Christ would — nay, does meet with the few faithful ones now as he did in the days of his earthly sojourn.
>
> Our personal knowledge of the unostentatious and modest Christian spirit of the brother who sends the donation and writes the words of encouragement, causes me to believe he would prefer his gifts were not published to the world, so we suppress his name.
>
> She also sends me a letter from a brother from Ala., stating that while he is poor, not able to give money, if he can find work to enable him to make a living, he would be glad to make his home with them to aid them in the worship. This too is a most commendable spirit. So often Christians like to go where the cause is popular, where they can find society and friends at church with nothing to do. The true spirit ought to be, I wish to go where I can do most good, where I am most needed, where the cause is weakest.
>
> If this spirit which was in Christ and Paul and is the true spirit of Christ, dwelt in all Christians, the weak places would

grow strong and the desert blossom as the rose. Brethren let us all cultivate this spirit. Mrs. A. F. McMullen,

Dear Sister —Enclosed please find check on New York for $25 which I send as contribution, to aid in building your chapel. I beg to assure you that I would consider it a greater privilege to sit down at the Lord's table, with those 15 sisters, "eight of whom are widows," than to occupy "a platform seat" in the largest and finest church in the universe.

It is my faith that if our blessed Savior were here on the earth now, that he would visit that faithful little band at Huntsville. You rejoice often doubtless, in the message he left for you. "Fear not, little flock, for it is your father's good pleasure, to give you the kingdom." I am like Bro. Barnes. I admire your "pluck, faith and zeal." You are bound to succeed. I do not believe any congregation ever failed of the Lord's blessing if faithful in attending his appointments. With my best wishes for all, I am your brother in Christ.[101]

Lipscomb also, like Barnes, admired Christians who stood strong on the scriptures. One can see that he admired sister McMullen's courage and faith.

Negative reactions to the situation in Huntsville were disturbing to—especially the ladies who had struggled so hard and for so long a time to get a suitable house of worship built in Huntsville. This negative letter may have helped the cause in Huntsville. Efforts by various Christian workers from various parts of North Alabama eventually succeeded in securing a house of worship in Huntsville. By December, the construction was underway and the Huntsville paper *The Mercury* published the following:

> One hundred and thirty thousand bricks are on the vacant lot opposite the Federal Court building, for the Christian Church. We are glad to note the beginning of the work; and we shall take

much pleasure in chronicling the completion of the much-needed church edifice in our city.[102]

One of the editors, at the *Gospel Advocate*, wrote a footnote to this announcement:

> We hope the work will be rapidly pushed forward to execution. We rejoice with these brethren in this bright prospect of a church house so soon. They have struggled faithfully and will soon reap the reward that faithful work always brings.[103]

Another letter was written by an Indiana transplant—Bro. J. C. Ferris. He also wrote about the congregation and their building of a house of worship. The letter was written on December 11, 1886, but was not published until a month later:

> Dear Brother Krutsinger, I have thought several times of dropping you a line as I doubt not, you will be glad to hear from me once more. I am not a recalcitrant, but true to the teachings of the word of God. You doubtless will remember when I call your attention to the fact of your once saying to me at our schoolhouse on Chestnut Ridge, "Bro. Ferris, you ought to preach more. Well, I do preach more now than then, but yet I am not considered a preacher. We have a small congregation here of true and faithful disciples. We are striving to build a house to meet in. We have a very handsome lot presented by Bro. H. (Hundley), and the brick are all on the ground preparatory to putting up the building in the Spring. But we are all poor with one or two exceptions. There are but few members. The congregation is principally females, mostly widows. But we trust that we will succeed in getting up and finishing our house next summer. We do not fail in our Lord's day meeting. We look for about the same number that are faithful and true to their duty each Lord's day. I am doing the best I can to instruct them in the absence of a better teacher. Occasionally we have calls by some of our

preaching brethren, but not often. If you should ever at any time visit our state, do not forget Huntsville and your old friend and brother. In the hope of the gospel.

J. C. Ferris, Huntsville, Ala., Dec. 11, 1886, formerly of Chestnut Ridge, Ind.[104]

Like all other letters written before, concerning this work, we see a pattern. They all mention the small size of the congregation and being composed mostly of widowed women.

In June of 1887, Andrew Perry wrote of an unusual memory he had of the congregation in Huntsville:

> How often when I learn this of a congregation, do I think of the dear brotherhood at Huntsville, Ala., where the clerk of the congregation kept a record of the Lord's day meetings and every absent one was aware that every absence was being marked against him. Andrew Perry.[105]

The years 1887–1889 were basically a quiet period as for much reporting on the work in Huntsville. Things changed in November of 1889. James A. Harding closed a meeting in Nashville went to Huntsville, Alabama, and began a meeting the last week of November.[106] The first report concerning this meeting was as follows:

> Advice from Huntsville, Ala., stated that Bro. Harding is getting on splendidly in his meetings, notwithstanding the competitions of the denominations. There were ten additions at last report, and the audiences were growing rapidly in both size and interest. Our people there, though few, are working zealously and a glorious meeting is confidently expected.[107]

The dream of having their own house of worship finally materialized in 1887. The house is still the home of the Randolph Street Church of Christ in 2024. The struggle was long and tiring;

but worth the struggle—thanks to the faithful women in Huntsville and especially sister Amanda McMullen with her untiring faith and hard work in leading the charge.

James A. Harding came several times to Huntsville and preached in extended meetings. He came in 1889 and held a successful meeting. By Christmas, it was reported that:

> Bro. Harding has entered the fourth week of his meeting at Huntsville, Ala., With an immense audience. There have been twenty additions to date. This is a good meeting, and we hope the meeting will grow to still greater interest.[108]

This information was given by a brother Hundley (most likely Orville M. Hundley) of Huntsville, who had visited the office of the *Gospel Advocate* on the Thursday before Christmas of 1889.[109] The final report was not published until January 1, 1890. The total number of additions was twenty-two.[110]

Then came one whose motives were purely divisive. The missionary society craftily raised its ugly head in Huntsville in the spring of 1890. This occurred through the labors of O. P. Spiegel, one of Larimore's former students, who, after Mars Hill, went to the College of the Bible in Lexington, Kentucky. That school was, by then, controlled by the missionary society crowd. He came with his usual tactics of preaching things the congregation was accustomed to hearing; and gaining their confidence, then he would slowly introduce ideas leaning toward the missionary society. He would eventually cause division and sometimes turn most members to his way of thinking. When that occurred as it happened in Selma, Alabama in 1906, the brethren who followed the New Testament pattern were put out of their new building. His visit in May of 1892 was just the beginning of trouble for the little band in Huntsville. His progression through his method can be seen as the reader begins to observe each visit to the church in Huntsville. The following note from Spiegel seems harmless enough:

> Anniston, May 1, '92. The writer preached four times in Huntsville, Ala., including last Lord's day and night. On Saturday night three young ladies made the confession and were baptized the same hour of the night in the Huntsville spring. We have a zealous band of disciples in that beautiful city, and they are struggling to get their house paid for they have stood firmly and worked incessantly in the past. Those who are able can give to no nobler work than that of helping these brethren out of debt that their fondest hopes to have a house of their own in which to worship God may be realized. They have had a hard struggle. May the Lord sustain and strengthen them. Send contributions to Mrs. I. F. Collins, Huntsville, Ala. O. P. Spiegel.[111]

David Lipscomb revealed where Spiegel's sympathies were when he authored an article discussing a conversation between F. D. Srygley and Spiegel:

> ... In that conversation I understood him to say, as he declares above, that he advocated societies to draw him out, but is really opposed to them. It is a strange thing; he declares himself opposed to the society above, yet he is in the employment of the General Society and is President of the Alabama State Society. Bro. Speegle (he changes the spelling to Spiegle later) is young yet, we believe will grow in wisdom and prudence as he grows older. We wish him only good.
>
> Since publishing the above, I have learned Bro. Speegle has resigned his connection with both societies. We are glad to hear this, and, while we cannot see the least wrong done to him in the matter, we would be sorry to do him the least injury. D. L.[112]

Spiegel was not long disconnected from his society leanings. He soon was in full fellowship. He would devote the rest of his life to societies and their approach to evangelism. The missionary society, of which Spiegel was a part, made the claim that the Churches of Christ did not know how to evangelize. A case in point—Selma, Alabama in 1906. The congregation had built a new house of worship. As it was nearing completion, those who had been influenced by Spiegel wanted the instrument of music introduced in the new building, along with the society connections. Several objected but were eventually put out of the new building. Those in favor of the society made the claim to those leaving that they would show the non-society group how to evangelize. In 2006 the Disciples church closed its doors in Selma as their membership fell to three people. There were, at that time, seven congregations of the Churches of Christ in and around Selma and no congregations of the Disciples of Christ.

The society had ostracized T. B. Larimore by May of 1892. The *Gospel Advocate* complained about this action in a discussion with an editor of one of the society papers in Texas:

> Bro. Larimore has been in North Texas nearly three months during which time he has held at various places several grand meetings, but we have failed up to date to see any notice of them in the *Christian Courier*. This is a matter of surprise, as our Texas contemporary usually displays a very commendable enterprise in gathering news "from the field."[113]

Lipscomb was disturbed at the silence of the *Christian Courier* concerning the meetings held and the additions by Larimore's efforts. He continued:

> Bro. Larimore began work in Texas, in February. The Courier made no mention of him till May 4. During all that time he was laboring with splendid success at different points in the state, and several notices of his work appeared in the Advocate and other papers. Letters from Texas, from the Advocate and the Courier interpreted the Courier's failure to notice Bro. Larimore's work, as a boycott. Bro. Larimore himself did not complain. That long and painful silence is still unexplained.[114]

The reason this treatment of Larimore is mentioned here is that Larimore was so well-loved by the churches in Madison County that it affected the attitude of the churches there. The Christians were disturbed, and they were sympathetic toward Larimore. Even secular papers in Huntsville, conveyed the same sentiment as can be seen in the following article:

> The spirit of the age is decidedly opposed to denominational bigotry and partisan intolerance in religion. Public sentiment is against institutional religion and in favor of unsectarian Christianity. In evidence of this, the following editorial remarks in the Huntsville, Ala., Evening Tribune are submitted: Interest in the service at the Christian church is growing daily. Last evening there was a fine attendance. The impressive baptismal services were conducted, three people connecting themselves with the church. There is no tableau more beautiful, certainly none purer, and more elevating, than the beautiful scene presented when the individual is received into the Church of Christ through repentance, determination to lead a. Christian life, faith, and baptism. This beautiful picture was presented twice last night. None can witness It without bowing their heads In instructive, even deep reverence. Elder Larimore is a strong pulpit instructor. While an educated man, there is a rugged strength about him which constitutes the eloquence of logic. The people of Huntsville are standing in their own light when they fall to hear him. In fact, none but the blinded, the weak-minded will say, "I will only attend services at my own church." When people attain that high degree of selfishness and prejudice the devil has an off eye, If not a string tied to them. Just such bigotry as that, which Is oftener led by the ministers than otherwise, is what is bringing this country to its low standard. The editor of the Tribune has attended the services at the Christian church four times within a week. During those four visits we never saw a single minister representing the other denominations. In other words, they seem to be standing from under and

letting Elder Larimore make the fight for the redemption of sinners single-handed and alone. While we do not propose to give the ministers of this city a moral lecture and urge them to stand together for the Lord, and not like a balky team, one pull one way and another jerk the other, at the same time it does sound ugly to an outsider to hear each minister saying, let every preacher " tote his own skillet." We say to these gentlemen that the sensible object of man, the instinct of the intelligent being from the cradle to the grave, is to go to heaven when he dies. To reach this boon of earthly desires, he is not going to indulge in hair-splitting as to which denominational road he will travel. They will all do, and it makes him tired, to see preachers sulking and pulling against each other over slight immaterial differences of opinion as to the direction leading to heaven. If every minister in Huntsville were to report at the Christian church and say, "Brother, I am with you; If your church is not large enough, move to mine," you would see the largest revival of religion in this city ever witnessed. But when the other ministers sulk in their tents, shake their heads, and say, "On, no, that is not my way to do the thing, the rest of the world say to themselves, rather than to get into the squabble about doctrines, We will put the thing off just as long as possible for us to do so." In this way, and for this reason, many a poor fellow has been projected head foremost into a sizzling, cracking, popping hell, while the ministers were singing psalms and talking about orthodox differences as to wholly immaterial questions. If they would all preach Christ as the Savior of mankind in all of its simplicity and purity and quit kicking each other and the rest of the world, religion would take a stronger hold in this country.

Such editorials as the foregoing in the daily secular papers, backed up by such preaching as Brother Larimore always does, will command the attention, convince the judgment, and move the hearts of the people in spite of the indifference, or even against opposition, of religious partisan leaders. If the editor of the Tribune, however, will look more closely into this question of denominational roads to heaven, he will probably modify his opinion that "they will all do," and agree with Brother Larimore and the *Gospel Advocate* that none of them should be relied on. The better plan is to stand aloof from all factions, parties, denominations, sects, and schisms in religion, and be simply a Christian. There are no such parties or denominations in the New Testament, and there ought not to be any such things now. [115]

We do not know the religious persuasion of the editor of the *Huntsville Tribune*, but he was a believer in Larimore's message.

By 1895, during all this turmoil, the church was in a thriving condition. Not everything, however, ran so smoothly. The brethren wrote a letter denouncing a Madison County preacher, who just a short time before was getting praise for his work. We do not know what his offense was but he was censored by the elders at Huntsville as follows:

> To whom it may concern: The officers of the Church of Christ at Huntsville. Ala., at their regular monthly meeting, July 7, 1895, in the matter of the application of B. C. Goodwin, heretofore a preacher in North Alabama, and perhaps Tennessee, for a church letter. It was ordained and subsequently ratified by the church that the said B. C. Goodwin is unworthy to receive a letter or commendation, or to preach in the churches of Christ.
>
> [Signed] Elders O. M. Hundley, A. W. Mosley, Ira F. Collins. M. J. Collins, Clerk. [116]

Whether the brethren were right or wrong in the matter, we do not know. They did what they thought to be Biblical. Three years later Goodwin was restored at Paint Rock under the preaching of J. R. Bradley (the writer's great-great-uncle). J.R. authored the following report on the restoration of B. C. Goodwin:

> I am glad to inform you that our brother, B. C. Goodwin, who, some years ago, was mentioned or spoken of as a "disorderly walker," has made recently, at Paint Bock, Ala., an open and public confession of his wrongs. Brother Goodwin has done good work at Paint Rock in years gone by, and we hope and pray that he may lead an exemplary life in the future. J. R. Bradley, Gurley, Ala.[117]

Later we find Goodwin back in the field doing what the brethren thought was a very good job.

—A side note here on the letter of withdrawal by the Huntsville church: We note that the brethren addressed the church as "the Church of Christ at Huntsville. Ala." The reason for pointing this out to the reader is that the historical marker, standing directly in front of the Randolph Street building, reads — "In 1900, the members began to refer to themselves as the church of Christ." Randolph Street is the name given when the congregation built their building across the street from the U. S. Courthouse. It is clear the congregation used that designation at least five years before 1900. By the way—the building still standing is the original building.

Spiegle would not give his efforts up, just yet. He came back vigorously in his work in Alabama fully involved in the work of destroying good Bible-based churches in Alabama and turning them into very liberal society congregations. Spiegle had approached the still infantile church in Huntsville and tried to turn it but had failed in his effort. When the society came the instrument of music in worship always followed—and this was what was so repulsive to the brethren in Huntsville; at least most of the brethren, as we shall see. It seems that Spiegle's feelings had been hurt over the rejection, so he writes a nasty letter to the brethren in Huntsville.

Speegle and others had tried to bring Larimore into the denominational organization of the Christian Church. Lipscomb addressed this issue by publishing the following lengthy article:

Larimore to the denominational organization of the Christian Church. All such efforts have failed, and for that reason Brother Larimore has never been "in full fellowship and good standing" with organized effort. The following, letters —omitting date; address, and a few names indicate that partisans have tried to weaken his influence and hinder his work for God on the broad basis of undenominational New Testament Christianity:

"About one hundred and twenty present last night; best audience we have had; three additions yesterday — only eleven, all told to date. Brother____, of ____, one of the immortal five who formed the conspiracy and organized the boycott against me here, has been in town, very busy. Impossible to do much here, but I am resolved to do all the good I can____. Of the five leading conspirators who inaugurated the boycott against me here, ____, ____, and ____ have been on hand to help me in the fight. ____ and ____may be here; if so, I do not know it. Probably the saints think three of the immortal five and a host of the commoner sort can hold me down. We still have from thirty to fifty hearers, and some of them stay till the benediction is pronounced. Brother ____'s head is in the bloody basket. When the bosses order a boycott the bossed must boycott or be butchered. Well, we will just hold our breath, and see what we shall see. T. B. Larimore."[118]

Larimore's treatment from society supporters had given him all that he could take, and he fires back in a surprisingly un-Larimore way:

"Meeting closed. About ten or a. dozen additions. Never had an audience. Twice we had probably one hundred and twenty present, all told-viz., on the first Sunday night and last Sunday night. All for the worse, however. On those two nights many came after preaching began; stayed till the most critical and important moment in the discourse; and then stampeded. The leader of the mob must be a man or woman of experience and good judgment. In both cases the mob was composed of well-dressed-or, I should say, fashionably and stylishly dressed-people, who looked at a distance like white folks. Indeed, I had taken them for gentlemen and ladies but for their heathenish conduct. But for that heathenish mob I had not closed the meeting last night. However, I think it was best to close it. They might have used dynamite if they had failed to break the meeting last night.

The meeting has been —"However, some good has come of it. A few months ago, I was, I believe, leaning toward the Christian Church just a little. Possibly nothing but heathenish treatment, heroic treatment, could cure me. Well, ten months' —no, twenty-four months' treatment has cured me. I will never go to a movement — never!" T. B. Larimore.[119]

The more Spiegel did by way of trying to discredit Larimore the more popular Larimore became in the North Alabama area. It is evident by those who responded concerning this controversy started by Spiegel. The church at Huntsville responded as a strong congregation. Some of the elders, but not all, reacted. Individual members wrote statements, also, praising Larimore's reply to the open letter from the State evangelist of Alabama. Here are two examples:

Concerning Brother Larimore's reply to the open letter from the State evangelist of Alabama, Ira F. Collins, Huntsville, Ala., writes: "We all believe your reply to Brother Spiegel is the best thing ever written by any of 'our' scribes."[120]

Then the ever-faithful sister McMullen stated:

... Mrs. Dr. McMullen, Huntsville, Ala.: "Would that I could stretch my arm from Huntsville to Mars' Hill, take your hand in mine, and from the depth of my heart say: 'God bless you always and forever and eternally for your reply to Brother Spiegel's open letter.' I know he will."[121]

One can see that in Huntsville, very strong sentiments were in favor of T. B. Larimore and not O. P. Spiegel. The society members were set on introducing 'organs' into all churches if they could get away with it. Their greatest advocate for this, in Alabama, was Oliver Pickens Spiegel and he was very persistent in his work of disrupting churches from Huntsville to Mobile. This can be seen in his letter to the church in Huntsville. In October, the *Gospel Advocate* published an article concerning the effort of the missionary society and its supporters to place the organ in every congregation of the Church of Christ. This article contained the letter to the church in Huntsville as follows:

> In a correspondence with the church at Huntsville, Ala., last spring, Brother O. P. Spiegel, state evangelist of Alabama, and on the pay roll of "our general" society the last time I examined the minutes, explains how our general and State missionary societies "put organs into churches," under his administration as follows: I have a very fine singer who usually goes with me. We have some great meetings. Of course, some at first do not like our methods, not understanding us; but no one who hears us through fails to indorse us. Our only contract for a meeting is that we be allowed to run it as seems best to us, with the co-operation and advice of the church, and that entertainment be furnished us, and then for our support we take voluntary contributions of members and friends of the church of Christ .... If we want one, two, three, or a dozen songs before the sermon, we have them; if I want Professor —to sing a fine solo to impress a truth, I have it; if I want to have one stanza in the middle of my sermon to impress in song what I am teaching, I have it. Professor — uses an organ to fill up weak places and hold all voices steady. This is an age of progress, development, and enlargement — He [God] ordained that his people should use instruments of music in the old economy [Old Testament]; they were never condemned in the new; they are used to illustrate the highest type of heavenly music and holy service in the world to

come. In view of these facts and others, suppose I should play a weak brother, and say they must be used, etc.; then how about Rom. 14:10-13; 15:1, 2? In answer to these passages see Acts 5:29. There is utterly no excuse for weak brothers in Huntsville in 1897, not if your eldership has done its duty. Of course, if it encourages weak brothers in their slothfulness and ignorance by putting a premium upon them, you may always expect to have such members. Yes, Brother Daugherty sung for you without the organ, but less than six months ago, on the streets of Nashville, he told me if the Lord would forgive him for using so much there, and several other places also, he would never do again. He said no sensible musician would conduct the music unless the church would let him conduct it, and that no musician would risk his reputation by affirming that you could get anything like as good music out of an audience without as with an instrument. I tell you this is an age of progress, development, and enlargement, and what Daugherty did when an inexperienced boy away back in the eighties is no sign of what he will do in the nineties. No, Professor would not sing without the use of an instrument. I have filed your letter for future use, as an official document from that church, refusing me the use of the house to preach in at my own charge. I stand thoroughly identified with the great bulk of the disciples who have fought so many battles and gained so many victories. When I make my report, they shall of course set about to have some preaching done in Huntsville, as there seems not to be a single church in the city which stands for free thought and free speech. You can communicate this message in full to the open congregation there, if that is a congregational church, as all the churches of Christ were in the first three centuries. O. P. Spiegel.[122]

After reading Spiegel's letter one can clearly see that his affection for the church in Huntsville had turned to anger when he was rejected. This was his typical mode of operation throughout his life.

The church survived that vicious attack and would move on, but the seeds of division had been sown there. The faithful leaders and members moved on with their work of evangelizing. They invited sound men to conduct meetings for them. In February 1898, the *Gospel Advocate* reported:

> Brother F. W. Smith has recently closed a good meeting at Huntsville, Ala., with twelve additions. He left Brother J. A. Harding to continue the meeting for a short time.[123]

During the same period, another report told of J. A. Harding's meeting. It reported that Harding had been engaged in the meeting for several days.[124]

Then others followed, holding Spiegle's work in check. F. D. Srygley came to Huntsville on the fourth Sunday of January 1899.[125] Granville Lipscomb had a good meeting at Huntsville, Ala., by the end of October 1899. There were twelve additions by the meeting's conclusion.[126] These were just a few of the preachers who came to Huntsville in its formative years.

The Disciple Christian Church movement finally gained a foothold in Huntsville as is shown in the following excerpt by the Watsons in their history of the Disciple movement in Alabama:

> The Disciples of Christ movement was launched in Huntsville, Madison County, July 13, 1947, when eight local residents and a delegation of supporters from Athens assembled in the Central YMCA auditorium. The three founders, Mr. and Mrs. John P. Mealing, Jr., and Mrs. Joyce Jones, led the group in seeking support for an organized church. J. A. Smoake of Athens and Robert Glenn of Valhermosa Springs with their churches sustained the Huntsville church through thirteen trying weeks. Another pillar of strength was Harrison McMains of Atlanta, who with Mrs. McMains made frequent visits.
>
> During the last three months of 1947 the church was formally organized as a project of the Crusade for a Christian

World. Wheels of the organization were set in motion by Percy E. Kohl, secretary-director of the Christian Churches of Alabama, and E. K. Beckett, regional evangelist for The United Christian Missionary Society. From October until December 1947, Mr. Beckett conducted two Sunday worship services at the YMCA.

The greatest long-range boon to membership came through a series of radio broadcasts designed to acquaint the public with the Christian Church and dispel confusion with the Church of Christ. The Church of Christ was known as the First Christian Church until 1948 when it became known as the Randolph Street Church of Christ.[127]

Liberalism was beginning to plague the little congregation. O. P. Spiegel's efforts at trying to turn the congregation continued; but the brethren were tied too closely to T. B. Larimore, as he was the first to plant the gospel seed in their midst. His relationship was too strong for Spiegel to drive much of a wedge between the Huntsville brethren and their love and respect for Larimore.

The work of Spiegle was stalled for nearly three-quarters of a century before it finally took root in Huntsville. Spiegle had been dead since February 6, 1947. He did more to take away the energy of the Restoration Movement in Alabama than any other person. The corridor from Athens, Alabama to Mobile (now basically the I-65 Interstate corridor) was his field of action.

It is hard to conceive how a man such as Spiegel, who had attended Mars Hill under Larimore, could be so mean-spirited toward a man with such a sweet spirit. Spiegel tried to nullify the influence, as well as that of J. M. Barnes of South Alabama. If Spiegel could do that, his battle would be won. Spiegle kept on trying throughout Alabama, to disrupt the momentum of the movement; but north Alabama was just too well established along the line of thinking that the early preachers had.

The work at Randolph Street continued to grow. The church had a gospel meeting in the middle of the summer. F. W. Smith, who was no stranger to the Huntsville brethren, came in July and held an extended meeting:

> Brother F. W. Smith has been in a meeting at Huntsville, Ala. There had been nineteen additions when we last heard from there, which was on the 13th inst.[128]

Things were going very well by the year 1901 and the church in Huntsville wished to share the condition of the church and did with the entire brotherhood. They sent a rather detailed letter to the *Gospel Advocate*, detailing the various aspects of the church's labors and good fortune; under the heading "The Church of Christ at Huntsville, Ala.":

> A Report. Dear Friend in Christ: Believing you to be deeply interested in the welfare and general prosperity of the church. for which our blessed Redeemer died, we take the liberty of addressing to you this personal letter, in which a report of work done and the present condition of the church of Christ is made, trusting that the facts herein stated will cause you to rejoice and thank God for the progress made and the privilege of taking part in the good work. It is furthermore believed that this report will stimulate and encourage us all to greater diligence, love, and sacrifice in the future than in the days that are gone.
>
> The law governing sowing and reaping is the same in grace as in nature. If we sow sparingly, we shall also reap sparingly. In view of this, we should remind each other of the words of our blessed Lord and of Paul. the apostle: "But this I say, He which soweth sparingly shall reap also sparingly; and he which soweth bountifully, shall reap also bountifully. Every man according as he purposeth in his heart, so let him give; not grudgingly, or of necessity: for God loveth a cheerful giver" (2 Cor. 9:6, 7.) Thus, we sow to the service of God our material substance and reap spiritual blessings. "It is more blessed to give than to receive."

(Acts 20:35). "I was glad when they said unto me, Let us go into to the house of the Lord." (Ps. 122:1).

From July 2, 1900, to the present date (April 1901) there have been thirty added to the church here, and the following figures show the various amounts raised within the same period: Preacher's fund collected. $234.62; preacher's fund disbursed. $200; general and Lord's day collection. $155.97; general expense. $182.91: total collected for preaching and general expense. $390.41; money collected to pay on indebtedness of the church, $420.20; total money collected and disbursed for all purposes. $814.61.

It will be seen from the above that the past ten months have been the most prosperous in the history of the church. Our regular receipts have more than doubled and we have had regular preaching four days in each month. Let us, therefore, feel encouraged to redouble our diligence, increase our labors, and unite our prayers to Almighty God for his guidance, that he will rule and ever rule in all our efforts to serve him and that the welfare of the church and the greatest honor to his name may be attained. Ira F. Collins, Jesse E. Boyd, Huntsville, Ala., Elders. [129]

In less than a year's span (July 1900–April 1901) the church grew by thirty new additions and doubled their contribution. No wonder the church was so happy and hopeful; but just when things are the best, it seems the devil enters the scene. A problem was brewing. It was yet in its infant stage but would be revealed within the next four years. In the meantime, the church enjoyed its labors.

It seemed that things were turning around for the spiritual condition in Huntsville. Brother C. Petty to Huntsville, Ala., during the year 1901.[130] He was a well-known evangelist throughout North Alabama and Middle Tennessee. No doubt he would help strengthen the already improving work. We find no reports of any meetings for 1901.

A brother W. J. Brown, of Cloverdale, Ind., came to Huntsville, Ala., on the third Lord's Day in March and preached in a meeting.[131] We have no report of any results for that meeting. In April F. W. Smith held a meeting that ended on the 14th that was described by the *Gospel Advocate* simply as "a good meeting."[132] That was not the end of the story—brother Ira. F. Collins—one of the elders wrote the following report of this meeting on June 16:

> Brother F. W. Smith has just closed a very successful two-weeks' meeting at Huntsville. Where were six additions- five baptisms. The singing was led by Brother Thomas Hales, assisted by Sisters Nannie Hales and Annie Draper, of Nashville, Tenn., and was much enjoyed and appreciated by the congregation.[133]

Nearly a year and a half after the first financial report, another report was sent to the *Gospel Advocate*. This report came in September of 1902, but it was not printed until the first week in October. The editors did print a brief statement about receiving it:

> We have received a very encouraging general and financial statement of the church at Huntsville, Ala. The statement embraces a period of twenty-six months, beginning on June 1, 1900, and ending on September 1, 1902. Compared with the preceding twenty-six months, an increase of one hundred and twenty-seven percent is shown. There has been considerable increase in attendance and membership as shown by the statement.[134]

Two weeks later the full report was printed under the heading of General and Financial Statement:

> The following is a general and financial statement of the church of Christ of Huntsville, Ala., for the twenty-six months beginning on June 1, 1900, and ending on September 1, 1902: Total

amount of money raised for all purposes, $1,625.65; total amount of money disbursed for all purposes, $1,606.06, (leaving a balance in bank of $19.59); number of sermons preached in the twenty-six months covered by this report, 169; number of additions to the church, 52; average weekly attendance of members, 34 1-3. (This does not include people who are not members of the congregation.) By comparing these figures with the twenty-six months immediately. preceding, we note the following gratifying increase: Increase of total amount of money collected, $971.65, or over 127 per cent; increase in number of sermons preached, 128, or over 300 per cent; increase in attendance per week, about 11 per cent; increase in number of additions to the church, 35, or over 200 per cent. These gratifying results we attribute, under God, to the faithful and efficient ministry of Brother F. W. Smith and the zealous united efforts of the church. We think this congregation may well congratulate itself on the showing made by this report -not in a spirit of vainglory, not that we have done all that we might have done, but that we have done, as well as we have under such adverse circumstances. This should stimulate us to attempt greater things for Christ and expect even greater blessings and increase from our Heavenly Father in the future than have been vouchsafed us in the past. Let us "sow bountifully, that we may also reap bountifully." Commending you all to God, and humbly trusting in his gracious watch care, and guidance, we are, your servants in Christ. J. P. Watts, J. B. Boyd, Ira F. Collins.
[135]

We note that another elder has been added to this report. Collins and Boyd were on both reports. Was a new elder added to the eldership since the first report or were only two of multiple elders named in the first report? Either way one can see that the church was growing stronger in Huntsville.

After F. W. Smith came to Huntsville and held the successful two-week meeting in April, a report was circulated that F. W.

Smith had become deranged. It was a case of misidentification. The *Gospel Advocate* a report by M. H. Northcross:

> We give the following notice from Brother M. H. Northcross: "A report which is being innocently circulated that F. W. Smith is deranged is false. It is H. W. Smith, a grocer, of Shelbyville, Tenn. F. W. Smith, our noted evangelist, of McMinnville, Tenn., is thoroughly balanced-in fact, one of the ablest preachers in the State. People have got mixed over the initials of these two men." Brother F. W. Smith was in our office on last Saturday. He preached at Huntsville, Ala., on last Lord's day. There were four additions. The meeting at Manchester, Tenn., was postponed on account of sickness. We feel that justice demands that this explanation be made.[136]

The concerned brethren were relieved especially in Huntsville. As they had grown to love and respect brother Smith. Then came 2 ½ years of deathly silence over the church in Huntsville, except for one published meeting which occurred in June of 1904. E. L. Cambron reported on his meeting in Huntsville:

> Huntsville, June 22. My meeting in Huntsville closed on last Lord's-day night with fine interest and a large congregation. There were twelve additions, and the brethren were much encouraged. Brother Clyde Gleaves was with me the last few days of the meeting. He is a. good preacher; he presents the truth in a clear and forcible way. I shall next go to Bedford County, Tenn., for a meeting. E. L. Cambron.[137]

Something was stirring in the congregation at Randolph Street. Then everything began to happen. First, a report that caught the brotherhood off guard:

> To Whom It May Concern.
> In view of all the circumstances surrounding us religiously,

we, the disciples of Christ who meet at the City Hall each Sunday in Huntsville, Ala., desire to make this public statement:

Without impugning the motives of any one in any action heretofore had in reference to our church troubles-which have caused a world of trouble and have been the cause offence antagonisms, the alienation of former friends, even to the disruption of the church we are fully persuaded that this state of affairs ought not longer to exist among any people who wish to do right.

We are further persuaded that we all, both the one side and the other, have not discharged our full duty to each other as Christians, and further, now state it is our desire to do our full duty toward all parties concerned. We wish to serve our God faithfully and to have that charity that covers a multitude of sins and hope that others may have that charity toward us.

There is no tribunal of men to whom we may appeal for an adjudication of Christian rights as between us, except by mutual consent of parties at variance; no one authorized by law to take cognizance of any question at issue and settle the differences; therefore, it behooves us that we do not infringe upon the spirit of grace.

We, therefore, place ourselves upon record as saying: That we are willing to cast all our troubles behind us, forgiving all who may in any way have done us any harm or injury, and asking the forgiveness of any and all whom we may have harmed; that we stand ready to meet with all who may be willing thus to do and to be to them for the future what we all ought to have been to each other in all the past; that we will continue to meet at the City Hall and invite all to meet with us who feel as we feel on this subject, and who are willing to act as we have indicated that we should act, until we shall, on these conditions, find a welcome at another place more suitable for meeting. "A house divided against itself cannot stand." Soldiers of the cross should stand together, for great in union there is strength. Let every Christian man and woman that belongs to the church of Christ set to his seal that God is true and join with us in manifesting the spirit of the Master, that his church may be edified and become a mighty power for good in this city.

Signed: J.P. Carlisle, W. F. Fulgham, and A. W. Moseley, elders, and thirty-two others.[138]

W. F. Fulgham was the younger brother of Amanda F. McMullen (the "F" for Fulgham). We know that Amanda was a very conservative woman who adored T. B. Larimore very much. She would have followed his convictions to the grave. Was her brother of the same persuasion? We ask this, wondering if W. F. Fulgham was as conservative as his sister. If so, does that mean he and the more conservative group went to the courthouse to meet and worship; or does that simply mean differences over opinions, and not doctrine divided the congregation? Just speculating.

Brother C. Petty visited the office of the *Gospel Advocate* in August of 1905 and there was no mention by Petty or the *Gospel Advocate* as to what had transpired in the church in Huntsville.[139] We are left with wondering and speculating. We know when things look the brightest, many times the devil will divide. That is his greatest tactic — "Divide and conquer."

Things must not have stayed in a disruptive state too long — E. L. Cambron came back and held another meeting that resulted in ten additions in June 1906.[140]

Few reports came from Huntsville. The problem erupted and hopefully healed soon after. One request for an answer came from Ira F. Collins concerning Romans chapter eleven:

> Brother Lipscomb: Please give our Bible class light on Rom. 11. Especially tell us who are referred to (verse 16) by the terms "first fruit," "lump," "root," and "branches;" also "olive tree" (verse 17) and "root" (verse 18). Some of the class take the ground that "olive tree" and "root" refer to Christ, while others believe those words refer to the Jews. Huntsville, Ala. Ira F. Collins.[141]

In typical Lipscomb style, an answer was given, apparently satisfactory to Collins. No further comments were requested by him on this section of Romans after Lipscomb's answer.

In November 1907, R. N. Moody of Albertville, Alabama, came and held a meeting at Randolph Street signaling that the storm had passed from the congregation and now it was moving forward in the Lord's work. His report is given in full:

> Brother R. N. Moody writes from Albertville, Ala., "On the fourth of this month I began a meeting with the Randolph Street congregation, Huntsville, Ala., which continued one week. As a result of the faithful teaching done privately and, in the Lord's, day service, seven persons were baptized. All of them were ready to obey when the meeting began, so not one of these additions could be said to be the result of my preaching. It is pleasant to work with a congregation that thus prepares for a meeting."[142]

Moody returned in 1909 and held another meeting at Randolph Street:

> Albertville, August 30.—My first meeting for this summer began on the 1st Lord's day in June, with the loyal disciples in Athens. The meeting continued over two Lord's days, with no visible results. The brethren there are having a hard struggle against many odds, but with good courage they are pressing on in the work. My next meeting began on the first Lord's day in July, with the Randolph Street church of Christ, in Huntsville. This meeting continued ten days and resulted in one baptism. This congregation has passed through much trouble but is now moving along in peace and harmony; and they come nearer manipulating all material that comes within their influence than any congregation I know of.[143]

This report gives the first mention of any trouble having been at Randolph Street since the letter published in the *Gospel Advocate* in 1905.[144] The disruption was kept very low-key for those years between 1905 and 1909 when Moody casually mentions it. It now looked as though the congregation was healed but that only lasted for a time. In 1916 T. C. Little of Fayetteville, Tennessee gave a closer look at the trouble that plagued the Randolph Street Congregation:

> This is the church that has attracted so much attention in the past, by the things which they have suffered in the way of strifes. contentions, and divisions. It is not my purpose to discuss those troubles, but to speak of the present situation as I found it while visiting and preaching for them once a month last year. However, it is well for congregations to look backward occasionally and note their mistakes and failures of the past, so they may go forward the better. Since congregations and individuals are heirs to the same things, therefore they are never so perfect but what some wrong appears, or even so bad that some good is not present This congregation is not an exception to the rule. I have known them ever since its organization and before. They are now. And have been all the while, faithful, true, and self-sacrificing Christians, both men and women among them. but they are not congenial and halve not dwelt together in peace. Some years ago, they divided. then after a while they united again. and for a short while, reports came from them that they were working harmoniously for the Lord. Soon the tempter came and sowed seeds of discord. and the leaven began to work, so that they were soon so unharmonious that another separation took place, a portion of the congregation going to the Masonic Temple to worship. leaving the others to worship in the house on Randolph Street. While I was preaching for these people as stated above, I visited and preached for those worshiping at the temple one Sunday morning and evening. I found in both congregations good, faithful men and women who deplore the conditions and are anxious to pursue the best course to allay any

in feeling that may exist among them and at the same time enable tem to worship God in spirit and in truth. After preaching for them a year and giving the matter much earnest, prayerful consideration, without any ill will or unkind feeling toward anyone. I believe separation was the proper solution of their troubles. The city is large enough for another congregation. It may require much patience, faithful long-suffering and many sacrifices before they enjoy the peaceful harmony and fellowship they desire; but if it will bring them into the presence of the Savior to hear him say to them, "Enter into the joy of thy Lord." it will more than compensate them for all they have endured. I do not believe they will dwell together in Christian love and fellowship as one congregation. I am sure there was a better feeling among these people when I gave up the work there than when I began, and I believe it will continue to grow better until they will recognize each other as coworkers in the Master's cause and rejoice at each other's success. May God help them to forget the things that are behind and "press toward the mark for the prize of the high calling of God in Christ Jesus."[145]

As one can see, trouble hung around for some time before harmony was restored. The church kept trying to rise above the problems. They contracted John T. Smithson to preach for them. The hiring took place in the latter part of November or early December of 1910.[146] Smithson was a young unmarried man, and this was one of his earliest labors with any congregation. He was noted for authoring lengthy reports with little substance, as far historians are concerned. His first report did, however, contain some useful information in it:

> ... Here in Huntsville the cause of Christ has been sadly neglected for some time. There has ever been some as true and faithful members here as you will find on the earth, but they have been without a leader to guide them in the way of Spiritual life till at times they would become discouraged and almost

willing to give up. The struggle, no doubt, has been hard and God has had a hand in the work. He has sifted Huntsville to find the faithful, and only a few remained in the sieve. These few have taken on new life. They are moving onward and upward and increasing in earnestness, zeal, and faith. They have put off hatred and evil and put on love and righteousness. They need the encouragement of all the faithful. We most earnestly ask to be remembered by the faithful in their prayers as we move on in this great work that lies out before us ...[147]

Smithson tried to find any ray of hope that could be found. He seemed overjoyed that E. L. Cambron of Winchester, Tennessee came and preached for the congregation on the first Sunday in June, and one came forward and made confession. Nothing was said about baptism; so, we are left to believe that whoever responded just confessed their sins. This was at least that positive act that Smithson for which he was looking. The *Gospel Advocate* referred to Smithson by saying that he "feels so good he has to talk about it."[148]

In August, another report came through the *Gospel Advocate* —"Growing At Huntsville, Ala." It was very wordy and did not contain much useful information on the congregation. We give the only paragraph that directly reflects upon the status of the Randolph Street church:

> In addition to the regular Lord's-day services, there is a prayer meeting during the week. This is a feast for the spiritual man. The strength of a congregation can be seen by observing the attendance at these prayer meetings.[149]

The next report on the work at Randolph Street came, not from Smithson, but Jarrett L. Smith who came to Huntsville, Ala., "and preached there three times on the first Lord's day in January —one time at each different place of worship."[150] Smithson never mentioned Smith's visit.

In February Smithson sent another report:

> Huntsville, Ala., January 13.—Our work at Huntsville is moving off well. We have brighter prospects for good work this year than we have had for some years in the past. The whole congregation has taken on new life. We have some changes made which make the congregation almost a new and reestablished one. The crowds yesterday were both large and attentive. John T. Smithson.[151]

What did he mean by "changes made which makes the congregation almost a new and reestablished one?" Did he mean the congregation appointed new elders and deacons, or did he mean they changed times of meetings? Just what did he mean? No explanation ever came.

By February he reported that "There have been six added by membership and one by baptism since the first of the year."[152] Note only one baptism. The others placed membership. It seems that things had improved so that people who had not formerly been a part of the congregation felt good about being members at Randolph Street.

Smithson reported on March 25:

> Huntsville, Ala., March 25.—Our work here is moving on, and we think that it is doing better than ever before. The interest is growing all the time, and that is a good sign that the work is doing better. We are looking forward for the fifth Sunday, as we are to have Brother Pittman with us on that day. We have planned to begin tent work in this town on the first of April. John T. Smithson.[153]

He was looking forward to having brother Samuel Parker Pittman preach on the fifth Sunday in June and also the tent meeting. Smithson, however, never did report on the meeting with Pittman. We know nothing about Pittman's success in

Huntsville. He never mentions the fifth Sunday meeting again. He did, however, report on a meeting by C. M. Pullias in May. The report was made as the meeting was in progress:

> The meeting that is now being conducted by Brother C. M. Pullias is growing in interest, and to date there has been one baptism. We are hoping to have a good meeting and that there will be a number to obey the gospel before the meeting is over. Brother Pullias is an able man and is doing some good preaching. The meeting is being conducted in a tent. At some services, the tent will not seat the people. Pray that the meeting will do much and lasting good. We need to stand by the work here faithfully. Another account will be given of the work here later.[154]

The long-anticipated tent meeting finally began. Smithson reported on this meeting as it was in progress. We note that he said that there would be another report to follow, however, Smithson never did send that follow-up report. Pullias made his own brief report "... a good meeting with two additions at Huntsville, Ala. [155]

On June 25, 1913, Smithson married Miss Bessie Welch. The report read:

> Married, at Huntsville, Ala., in the church of Christ, at 12:30 P.M., Wednesday, June 25, 1913, Brother John T. Smithson and Miss Bessie Welch. Brother Smithson is a young preacher, located with the Randolph Street church of Christ in Huntsville, and his bride is the daughter of one of the elders of the congregation. Brother S. P. Pittman performed the ceremony. The *Gospel Advocate* extends heartiest congratulations.[156]

This was the last mention of Smithson as being in Huntsville. The next time we hear from him he is in southern Alabama. Charles L. Talley, a Lincoln County, Tennessee, boy, was the minister for the Highland Park congregation in Montgomery —

three Sundays a month and Greenville, Alabama every fourth Sunday each month. He reveals the where-a-bouts of Smithson in his report on his work in South Alabama:

> ... At the time I went there (Greenville) the brethren had a well-located lot they paid seven hundred dollars for, and since that time we have struggled and prayed, and about the first of September 1913, we began the use of a very nice, commodious house of our own, that will after January 1, 1914, have an easy balance of seven hundred and fifty dollars unpaid. House fully worth two thousand dollars. Brother John T. Smithson at that time taking this work in connection with other points; I to give all my time to Highland Park... Charles L. Talley.[157]

Just as mysteriously as Smithson was hired in Huntsville, was just the same mysteriously the way he left Huntsville. Never an explanation—not a word about it. Was he hired because Bessie Welch was already in love with Smithson, or did she fall in love with him after his arrival in Huntsville? Was he hired because of Bessie's father being an elder at Randolph Street? Smithson did live in the same house as the Welch family, or so, it appeared from what Jarrett L. Smith wrote on his visit to Huntsville in 1913. The statement was — "I stayed with Brother and Sister Welch and Brother Beecher Martin, in the home of Brother John T. Smithson."[158]

Now that Smithson had left Huntsville, the question was how did the work progress at Randolph Street? C. Petty wrote the first report after Smithson moved to South Alabama. His report covered the three congregations now established in the Huntsville township:

> Huntsville, Ala., March 16.—Yesterday was a fine day here with all the congregations. The weather was ideal. Sam Pittman preached two strong sermons at Randolph Street Church, with fine attention and good crowds. J. D. Jones preached a fine

sermon to a good crowd in the new church house at Merrimac, with splendid attention. Brother Jones said he "dedicated" that church, sure enough. The writer was with the East Town congregation, with about the usual crowd, but had splendid attention. Taking it all around, the cause of the Master is improving. We want every brother and sister in this town to work and pray for great success here this year; and if we all work together in perfect harmony and go to see every brother or sister who fails to attend services, we will do a great work here. C. Petty.[159]

Sometime between the middle of March and the third week in April C. M. Pullias preached at Randolph Street, with two additions.[160] This was the last report on the work at Randolph Street for the year of 1914, which is the date we chose to stop our history of the North Alabama movement. It is the beginning of the First World War, which ushers in a new era of restoration history. By now the other two congregations in Huntsville were taking the forefront and our history will pick up with them.

NEW HOPE

Another congregation was established in the 1880s, at a place called Vienna which was located very near the town of New Hope. This was a forerunner of the New Hope work. What is puzzling, is that J. H. Morris, not to be confused with J. H. Morris of Tuscumbia, Alabama, who also was a gospel preacher, was preaching and lived in New Hope. Why did he not establish a congregation in his hometown, by 1880? The first report of any attempt to establish a congregation in New Hope came from the wife of J. H. Morris. We know that Morris was preaching at least by 1880 because he was reported to have preached in a gospel meeting, which seemingly established the Owens Crossroads congregation.[161] The first *Gospel Advocate* report came in 1888 —eight years after Morris' preaching at Owens Crossroads was reported. His wife made the first report on this new work at New Hope:

> Mrs. J. H. Morris writes from New Hope, Ala., Sept. 2, 1888: "By request I write to give you some items for the Advocate. Embracing the third Lord's day in August, Bro. B. C. Goodwin held a meeting in the little town Vienna, Madison county, Ala. Although an old place the gospel of the Son of God had never

been received there in its primitive purity. Some of the gentlemen of the place were induced by my husband to take the Gospel Advocate last year. Now every one of those men are members of the body of Christ. The claims of the gospel were presented so plainly during the meeting that they now have an organized body of twenty odd members, and a house of worship will be there in the near future. We think this is a triumph of truth over error and hatred for prejudice ran high. The week following the Vienna meeting, Bro. Goodwin preached a few days at Paint. Rock near there with ten added. We thank God for the truth, and the noble defenders of the same. My husband was called home by sickness in the family on the 25th of last month, from a meeting in South Pittsburg, Tenn. The prospects were good for a successful meeting. He is now in Red River county, Texas, trying to persuade men to become followers of Jesus. We are so lonely while he is so far away."[162]

By April of the following year, J. H. Morris was reporting on the death of a brother James Monroe Taylor. This account of Taylor's death included a history of the beginning of the work at New Hope. We give this report in full:

By request of the brethren at this place I write you of the death of Bro. James Monroe Taylor. He was born in Madison county, Ala., August 6, 1850, and died at his home in the same county, March 8, 1889, I have known him about twelve years, be loved to talk about the Bible and when asked why he was not a Christian, his answer would be "I cannot see how to get my feet on the Rock." About three years ago he became convinced of the sufficiency of the word of God for man's guide to all truth. I prevailed with him to take the Gospel. Advocate, he did jointly with Bro. Stone, hoping it would influence his wife (then a Baptist) to see differently. In June 1888 Bro. B. C. Goodwin held a meeting in the public-school house. They both came forward and were buried with Christ in baptism and arose to walk a new life, and truly 1t was a new life. Even those say so who opposed him most. But he was willing to brave all malice or bitter prejudice for the sake of truth. The little band of disciples at New Hope made him superintendent of building the house for them to worship in under their own vine and fig tree. He had the building framed when he took cold, was prostrated on his bed with pneumonia never to rise until the resurrection morn "when that which is sown in weakness will he raised in power." May God bless and comfort sister Taylor, and oh that she may live to teach her boys to imitate their good father, is the prayer of the writer, J.H. Morris.[163]

It seems that B. C. Goodwin had been preaching in meetings for some time. He had held a meeting in June of 1888 and another in August of the same year at the Vienna schoolhouse, which eventually became the New Hope congregation.

Morris had mentioned the building of a meeting house in the obituary of James Monroe Taylor. He had made an appeal for help to finish the building. He made another appeal in June 1889. He appealed to the brethren by using scripture as an encouragement to solicit aid to finish the building. The request reads as follows:

> J. H. Morris writes from New Hope, Ala., June 3: "Some time ago I made an appeal for help to build a house of worship at this place. One sister sent one dollar: Sister Smith of Jackson, Tennessee. May God's richest blessings be hers through time and eternity, for she, like the widow has given more than they all. Now, shall this second "cry for help be in vain," and let the workmen carry the keys of the house? The outside of the house will be done in a few days. We lack about fifty dollars paying for it so far. But oh, how we desire to have the ceiling and inner part finished comfortably, not attractive, before winter. We will not let the workmen keep the keys. But, dear brethren, if we lift the load unaided by others, we can have but little preaching in the

house for some time, for they could not reward the laborer and this would cause pain in the body, and the Holy Spirit says if one member suffer all should suffer with it. How many good brethren and sisters will this reach who are willing to let the Lord open their hearts as he did Lydia's, and when this is done there is no difficulty in opening their pocketbooks, for Jesus says, "it is more blessed to give than to receive." And he that hath pity on the poor lends to the Lord. Send all to J. F, Ellet, New Hope, Madison county, Ala."[164]

In 1901 Charles L. Talley came to New Hope and held a meeting—beginning "September 7, laboring until September 16, with three confessions and baptisms."[165]

The next information on New Hope comes in 1906, in a report on R. N. Moody's meeting —reported by U. D. Ellett. Let us look at the report on Moody's meeting in September 1906:

> New Hope, September 20.—Brother R. N. Moody, of Albertville, has been at New Hope sowing the seed of the kingdom. Brother Moody is a true, tried, faithful servant of God, and knows just how to handle "the sword of the Spirit." As a result of his preaching, seven were baptized. North Alabama, and especially Madison County, is practically a mission field. U. D. Ellett.[166]

It was announced in the *Gospel Advocate* that Moody was engaged in a meeting at New Hope, in August 1907.[167] Details of this meeting were given in the first issue of the *Gospel Advocate* for September:

> Albertville, August 16. Our meeting at New Hope closed last night. The attendance and interest were good throughout the meeting. There were seven baptisms. Brother G. A. Dunn held a meeting here six or seven years ago. A fourteen-year-old girl who is a deaf mute attended his meeting, and from his chart

learned the requirements of the gospel and declared her intention to be baptized. Her mother, who was a Methodist, asked her how she knew Brother Dunn preached the truth. She replied: "I read it on his chart, and I came home and read it in the Bible just like it was on the chart." Her mother was very considerate and invited Brother Dunn to come to her house and talk with her daughter about the matter. Brother Dunn went and taught her "more perfectly" and before the close of the meeting she made the confession and was baptized. During the meeting just closed I had the pleasure of baptizing her mother and sister. If Brother Dunn could witness the happiness of this young lady on account of her mother's and sister's obedience, he would feel amply rewarded for all the pains he took to teach her duty. This incident shows how simple the gospel is to a mind that is unclouded with traditional religion. It was fortunate for this girl that she had never heard the sectarian jargon of the day. Again, it is an encouragement to faithfulness under all circumstances. Brother Dunn held that meeting under trying circumstances and in the face of much opposition, but the salvation of that one girl is worth the effort of the lifetime of any man. Again, it shows that all can do something. If this girl, who can neither hear, nor speak, can be instrumental in leading others to Christ, what ought we who are blessed with hearing and speech do? Her zeal for the salvation of others is not limited to her own people, but with pencil and tablet she is taking advantage of every opportunity to talk to others about obeying the gospel Her beautiful, childlike faith is an inspiration to all who see it to do more for the cause of Christ. R. N. Moody.[168]

Moody revealed that G. A. Dunn had preached at New Hope in the beginning of the work there. The meeting had been an interesting one, to say the least.

Moody returned in a meeting in August of 1908. This meeting was finally closed after twenty-two days of incessant rain, however, with thirteen additions to the church at New Hope. Because of the details, the report is given in full:

> Albertville, August 31.—I began a meeting with the congregation at New Hope, Madison County, on the second Lord's-day in August and continued it twenty-two days. The immediate result of the meeting was thirteen baptisms. Notwithstanding the fact that we were surrounded with denominational meetings almost the entire time, we had good crowds at every service, except three or four during the last week of the meeting, and even then, the attendance was not at all discouraging. This meeting demonstrated the fact that we too often close meetings too soon. We had only one addition the first week of the meeting; and had we closed then, that would have been all the result of the meeting, as far as additions are concerned. I am sure that the meeting could have continued with good interest and results for a month longer. The church here has put in a nice baptistery, which saved several long and tiresome trips to the river, a mile and half away. R. N. Moody.[169]

At the end of the fall of 1908, Moody reported on his evangelizing efforts for the year. He spoke more on the work at New Hope:

> From Langston I went to New Hope, where we began a meeting on the second Lord's day in August and continued twenty-two days, with thirteen baptized. This is one of the best working congregations in North Alabama, which is due largely to the untiring zeal and energy of one man. It is for the lack of such men that the cause is lagging in so many places. If every member of the church realized that his own salvation depended on his working for the conversion and salvation of others, we would soon have strong congregations in every community.[170]

These meetings strengthened the congregation and empowered it to be more concerned and do more for the surrounding area. Note New Hope's willingness to aid in a financial way with the groundwork for a congregation at Owen's Crossroads. So, the New Hope church began trying to evangelize the surrounding communities, as can be seen in the next report, written by R. N. Moody:

> I am now in a tent meeting near New Hope. The meeting is two days old, and there has been one baptism. This is the first of three mission meetings that the church in New Hope will help me to conduct, besides a meeting with the church. R. N. Moody.[171]

Moody sent a follow-up report:

> Albertville, September 5.—I have just closed a six-weeks' work with the church at New Hope. 1 first held four tent meetings in a radius of five miles of New Hope, or a week's length each, and then a two-weeks' meeting with the congregation in New Hope, There were eight baptisms in all these meetings. Many heard the word who had never heard it before, and seed was sown that will bear fruit by and by. The church at New Hope is not strong numerically or financially but supported the work reasonably well. They have capable and liberal leaders who have "a mind to work." Many congregations could do the same work, and would do it, if they were not handicapped by inefficient and stingy leaders. Such work will do more to settle the question as to how to do missionary work than all the debating we may do. God hasten the day when Christians will work more and debate less. R.N. Moody.[172]

In August 1911 Charles L. Talley came and held the August meeting at New Hope. Talley was one of those preachers from the Fayetteville—Lynchburg area who had been encouraged by J.D. Floyd, T.C. Little, and J.R. Bradley to preach. He became a very popular preacher throughout the southern states. The brethren at New Hope loved him and called upon him for gospel meetings, more than once. Talley gave us a snapshot of the work at New Hope in his report on this meeting:

> New Hope, August 28. Our meeting at this place is moving off well. We have entered the second week, with one confession to date and splendid prospects for a number of others. We seldom see an interest equal to that shown here. The house is, ordinarily, large enough to accommodate the crowds that attend the services, but at this time the house would be easily filled were it one-third larger. New Hope is a nice village of two hundred people and is surrounded by an ideal country. The congregation is loyal and one of the best-working small congregations in my knowledge. I held a meeting here eleven years ago, when I baptized some of those that are now leading in this good work, I rejoice in that fact and praise the Lord for the good work being done here. Brother R.N. Moody of Albertville has done much service in and around this place, and he is highly esteemed by the church for his work's sake. My next meeting will be in Franklin County, Tenn. Charles L, Talley.[173]

Brother G. A. Dunn came and preached in a gospel meeting in 1912.[174] No report was published on this meeting. We might assume that there were no results, or at least no visible results—preachers hardly ever reported having no results in their work.

Union Grove

Another congregation that began in the New Market area before 1900 was the Union Grove church. A few reports on this work were found in the *Gospel Advocate*. The first was written by R. J. Hastings. Hastings was an early force in causing the work to begin at Union Grove. Andy Largen wrote of him—"It was by his influence and that of a few others that the Union Grove church of Christ was established, and we may say for this church that it has done some very substantial work for the Lord."[175] Hasting's report gives the first look of the work at Union Grove:

> As I have not noticed anything in the Advocate from Union Grove in a long time, I want to tell you our little band is still alive. We have preaching once a month by Bro. E. L. Cambron. There were three added to the church second Lord's day in this month, two from the Presbyterians and one by confession and baptism. Many more are almost persuaded. We hope to be able to build a house for worship this fall. R. J. Hastings, New Market, May 15, '90.[176]

This snapshot of the early work reveals that the congregation was planning to build a house of worship. That demonstrated that the congregation had intentions of working and growing. It also reveals, by the absence of a meeting house, that Union Grove was a very new work. This would place the establishing date at about 1889 or 1890. The building, however, was not finished anytime soon. The church was forced to meet in borrowed buildings of denominational groups that would cooperate with them.

In August 1891, B. C. Goodwin stopped at an unscheduled stop and preached for the congregation. R. J. Hastings reported this stop to the *Gospel Advocate*:

> New Market, August 26,' 91. —Bro. B. C. Goodwin on his way from Well's Hill home stopped here at Union Grove and delivered five discourses, resulting in five additions by confession and baptism and one from the Missionary Baptists. R. J. Hastings. [177]

News about the work came in small bits and not often. About two years later a report was published in the *Gospel Advocate* in in August of 1893:

> Brother E. L. Cambron and I closed a meeting at Union Grove today, which resulted in ten baptisms and two putting away the unscriptural name of Baptist and taking upon them the scriptural name of Christian.[178]

J. D. Gunn sent the report in conjunction with the cooperative efforts of J. D. Jones of Madison County and E. L. Cambron, who was a well-known preacher from the Fayetteville, Tennessee area. From this report, we see that the church at Union Grove was growing numerically and that they were attempting to grow spiritually. Brother R. J. Hastings wrote to Lipscomb about a question that arose in the Bible study class at Union Grove:

> Brother Lipscomb: What did John the Baptist baptize for? The question was asked in our class at Union Grove. Some said he

baptized for the remission of sins. I do not understand the scripture that way. New Market, Ala., R. J. Hastings.

Mark 1:4—John did baptize in the wilderness and preach the baptism of repentance for the remission of sins. I could not make that plainer.[179]

Lipscomb's answer was short and to the point. This does demonstrate that Union Grove was trying to understand the Bible and brother Hastings was a spiritual leader in that congregation. In his obituary, Andy Largen, wrote this about Hastings:

> Brother Hastings served as an elder in the church for twenty-eight years, and his sincerity in life and proper attitude toward all questions caused the entire community to have great regard for him. R. A. (Andy) Largen.[180]

Not only did Hastings help establish Union Grove; but he was also a spiritual leader as an elder for the congregation. His death left a huge gap in the work at Union Grove in the following years.

From 1894 until June of 1897, there was no correspondence from Union Grove. J. R. Bradley held a meeting at Union Grove about which he wrote a short line: "August, to embrace the fourth and fifth Sundays, at Union Grove, Ala."[181] For some unknown reason, J. R. never reported the results of his meeting at Union Grove, which was so untypical of him.

It was seven more years before we found any more information on that congregation. E. L. Cambron was to begin a meeting on October 16, 1904.[182] Cambron, like J. R. Bradley, never reported the results.

The next mention of Union Grove came nine years later. J. J. Horton of Elora, Tennessee wrote: "I shall begin a two-weeks' tent meeting next Lord's day — [September 16, 1913] —at Union Grove, Ala."[183] That is all that we learn from Horton. Did he hold the meeting, or did he forget to report it? Were the results too meager to report? It is interesting that the last three preachers to report on meetings were only their expressed intentions to hold a meeting at Union Grove.

From this time forward for many years only a few reports came from Union Grove and this trend continued well into the 1930s. The congregation still exists and is among the oldest churches of Christ in Madison County.

Madison Cross Roads

The Madison Cross Roads work is more than one congregation; but an area in which multiple churches were established, mainly because the central focus was on the work beginning at the Cross Roads. The earliest mention of this work was from a report sent to the *Gospel Advocate* in May of 1890. The name was even misspelled as "Marion Cross Roads" instead of "Madison Cross Roads." There was never a Marion Cross Roads in Madison County, Alabama—it was simply a printer's error, and nothing more. L. B. Jones of Huntsville gives an account of his conversion and his first efforts at preaching, which included Madison Cross Roads. We give his report in full, as it is the first information on the Madison Cross Roads work:

> Since I joined the church of Christ, I have not been idle. I held services at Marion (Madison?) X Roads the third Lord's day in April; had a good congregation. I also held services on the fourth Lord's day, morning and evening, with a good congregation and good attention. Through my feeble efforts to preach the truth, at the close of the service three came forward and joined the church. I have an appointment for the first Lord's day in June. I hope I will be able to do some good in the vineyard of the Lord.

I am well pleased with the *Gospel Advocate*. L. B. Jones, Huntsville, May 19, '90.[184]

This is our first view of the work in this area. Later there would be other congregations established in a few years—especially the churches at Toney and Friendship.

J. H. Morton and J. R. Bradley, perhaps the first preachers to show interest in this community. Of these two men, Morton is the earliest to send a report on the Cross Roads: He simply states: "I will visit, the Lord willing, Madison Cross Roads, Ala., and McMinnville, Tenn., in the near future. J. H. Morton."[185] In his report, Morton states his intentions to preach there, but no report on his effort ever became known. We do not know if he came and preached or not. At this time in Madison Cross Roads, beginning the congregation, like most other congregations, met sporadically. They were not even a true congregation yet. They were a community with many scattered families who had been converted, such as L. B. Jones had been.

J. R. Bradley gives a picture of this very situation:

Fayetteville, August 10. On the second Sunday in July, I visited the County Line congregation. We had a favorable hearing. On the third Sunday in July, I began what was expected to be a week's meeting at Toney, Ala.; but I preached only four times, on account of the rain, though I remained with them all week. There are several members there who are certainly strong in the faith of the ancient gospel; but they do not so much need teaching upon the Lord's day work as they need a wonderful stirring up on these things. They are, with a little help, able to build a house of worship, such as would answer all purposes; but I think, since they have unmolested freedom in the use of a nice and commodious schoolhouse, it would be better to get into the habit of faithfully meeting and worshiping the Lord upon the Lord's day, as well without as with a preacher, and then look to the building of a house. J. R. Bradley.[186]

J. R. gives another report on this meeting in October:

> Fayetteville, October 3. Our meeting at Toney, Ala., which began on the third Sunday in August and closed on Friday night following, resulted in two people being baptized. We could hold preaching only at night after the Lord's day on account of the school. ... I am preaching now almost every Lord's day and Lord's day night. My health is very much improved, though I am not entirely well. My preaching is done nearly all the time at destitute places, and hence sometimes I do not get traveling expenses. This is exceedingly hard for one who has spent so much, and for so long, trying to get well. J. R. Bradley.[187]

In the latter part of Bradley's life, he battled kidney disease and that was compounded with malaria he had contracted in North Mississippi. He, at this period of life, was grateful to be able to preach anytime. His health held out well enough to return to this community several times and help the Toney-part of the work to get a proper grounding in their duties as Christians.

Bradley came again in the fall of 1907. The *Gospel Advocate* reported:

> Fayetteville, August 10. Our meeting at Toney, Ala., began on the fourth Sunday in July and closed on the first Sunday night in August. There were three confessions and baptisms, one restored, and one took: membership. Large audiences attended the services. Brother A. H. Rozar, of Fayetteville, and I did the preaching. Brother A. L. Dixon, of Coldwater, was there in a singing school, which was a help to our meeting. J. R. Bradley .... [188]

He also returned along with A. H. Rozar in July of 1908 for a meeting. The *Gospel Advocate* reported — "Brother J. R. Bradley is now engaged in a meeting at Toney, Ala."[189] Another report on the same meeting came in August of that year. It gave more details on these meetings, as follows:

> Brethren J. R. Bradley and A. H. Rozar are now in a meeting at Molino, Lincoln County, Tenn. They recently closed a meeting near Madison's Cross Roads near Toney, Ala., with two baptisms. They had the largest attendance the brethren have ever had at a tent meeting at meeting at that place.[190]

A note of interest on Rozar —A.H. Rozar and his son Vernon Rozar lived at Stoney Point, Moore County, Tennessee. Bradley had converted A.H. Rozar from the Separate Baptists in July of 1893.[191] A. H. Rozar had labored with J. R. in many meetings. J. R. said of the Rozars... "both splendid preachers and loyal to the cause of Christ."[192] Vernon would come to Toney-Madison Cross Roads area in 1924. Vernon Rozar wrote of this meeting:

> As results of my last two meetings, one was restored and one baptized; but one week following my meeting at Friendship, Ala., Brother Knowles, of Huntsville, preached for a week, and seventeen were baptized ....[193]

This report on Vernon Rozar helped highlight J. R.'s influence on the Toney work —both directly and indirectly through men he had helped train. Another "trainee" of J. R.'s was Charles L. Talley from the Lincoln-Marshall County area who was heavily influenced by Bradley. He came and held a meeting at Toney in the Fall of 1911. The *Gospel Advocate* reported this effort:

> Brother Charles L. Talley recently closed an eight-days' meeting at Toney, Ala., with eight baptized. The interest and attendance throughout the meeting were good. It is likely that the brethren will build a meetinghouse at Toney at an early date.[194]

Talley returned for other meetings. By this time Toney was a well-functioning congregation. In 1914 another preacher's name appears in the list of men who preached in the early days at Toney. He was A. D. Rogers. The following was reported by A. D. Rogers:

> Toney, Ala., March 25.—I preached last Lord's day morning at the new church, called "Sharp's Chapel," four miles east of Toney. Only twelve members were present, but we are hoping to strengthen the cause at this place. Brother Albright built most of the house, so he could have a place to meet and worship each Lord"s day; but he died just before the house was completed, and the few brethren are left to fight the battle alone. May God bless them in their efforts. A. D. Rogers.[195]

The work at the Cross Roads seemingly evolved into the Toney and Friendship congregations and the Madison Cross Roads ceased to exist. As for the Sharp's Chapel, four miles east of Toney, this is the only reference found in the *Gospel Advocate*. We do not know if that was a borrowed denominational building, which was common in those days in communities that had no building for the church of Christ, or was it a small community by that name. We are left to wonder.

Owen's Cross Roads

The Owen's Cross Roads community is more than just Owen's Cross Roads by itself. It is another area similar to the Madison Cross Roads area. Several families live around Owen's Cross Roads. The people designated their settlements by name; but when outsiders came in, they referenced those locations by how far they were from Owen's Cross Roads. Some of the very earliest work was done by J. H. Morris of New Hope, which, by the way, was just under six miles from Owen's Cross Roads. One reason for the work at the Owen's Cross Roads may have been because these larger settled communities had different denominations already in them. These denominational groups laid every roadblock before our brethren; therefore, they went to the surrounding areas first. After those outlying areas were evangelized, some of the people from those communities moved into larger communities, such as Owen's Cross Roads. This area began to organize into an economic center for that part of the valley, thus allowing our brethren more freedom to evangelize in these communities.

J. H. Morris of New Hope, Madison County, Alabama came into the Owen's Cross Roads area and held a mission meeting. He wrote on November 11, 1880:

> The fifth Lord's Day in October I preached near Owens X Roads, Madison county, in a new schoolhouse, in which the wife of Bro. Mathewson confessing the Lord and being baptized. She for many years was a devoted Methodist. I baptized her husband four years ago; since that. time he has been a devoted and zealous disciple of Christ. He has patiently borne the persecution of his neighbors and malice from the sects. But thank God, prejudice is giving way, and many are almost persuaded to be Christians. If any of the preaching brethren pass that way, please stop and preach for them, they will be well cared for.[196]

For some reason, it would not be until 1907 before an effort was made in the Owen's Cross Roads community. This work eventually merged with Owen's Cross Roads—that, however, would be a few years later. This report gives the background to the establishment of the church at Owen's Cross Roads. This possibly could have been the first sermon ever preached in that whole area. Brother Mathewson may have lived there or in another community and was just there with his wife to support brother Morris' effort in the Owen's Cross Roads area. Maybe in the future, this can be answered.

Through the influence of U. D. "Boss" Ellett, R. N. Moody finally came to the Owen's Cross Roads community and began preaching.[197] Moody's first report on this effort is given in full:

> Albertville, September 2. On the third Lord's day in August, I began a meeting at Owens' Cross Roads, Madison County, and continued it one week. The attendance was good throughout the meeting. There were five people baptized and one from the Baptists. Among those baptized was a young Baptist preacher who bids fair to make a good gospel preacher. This was the first preaching ever done there by our brethren. From the character of the material added, we anticipate a working congregation in the near future, We would have continued the meeting longer had it not been for a Methodist meeting beginning in a hundred

yards of the tent. They had postponed their meeting on our account, and we thought it best not to create any friction by continuing our meeting while theirs was in progress. This meeting was gotten up by the New Hope congregation, who intended to support it financially; but it was only necessary for them to make a small contribution to it, as a few brethren and friends of the community contributed to the support of the meeting. However, the New Hope congregation helped much with their presence. Almost the whole congregation was there on the first day of the meeting; and some of them were there at every service, notwithstanding the distance of six miles. We intend holding another meeting there about October 1, and anticipate more additions, as many others were much interested. I am now in a tent meeting in West Gadsden. So far, the attendance is fine. R. N. Moody.[198]

This shows the strong determination of the people in that community to "stand on their feet," if possible. They were to be admired for that mentality.

Moody came a year later and held his second meeting at the Owen's Cross Roads. He reported this meeting in November to the *Gospel Advocate* but he reflected heavily back on the previous meeting in 1907. His report read:

My next meeting was at Owen's Cross Roads, in Madison County. This meeting began on the second Lord's day in September and continued until the fourth Lord's-day night and resulted in eight baptisms. This was an important meeting because of its being at a very important new point in the midst of a sectarian stronghold. I held a meeting there last year, which was the first ever held there. Owing to circumstances over which we had no control, we were forced to close it too soon. At that meeting there were five additions, which, together with the additions of this last meeting, gives them a nucleus for a good congregation, which they may have if they are faithful. The congregation at New Hope intended to support the work there financially, but the contributions there last year and this were considered sufficient without their help, which shows us that destitute places are not always to be feared from a financial standpoint. In that matter my experience has been that such places, as a rule, contribute more liberally, according to their means, than many large congregations. R. N. Moody.[199]

From these two reports, a year apart, we gather that the work began in 1907 with difficulties. In this report, Moody said that they "were forced to close it too soon." He also said that the second meeting was important "... because of its being at a very important new point in the midst of a sectarian stronghold." So, the congregation became large enough to start meeting on a regular basis.

Two family names began coming to the forefront—Ellett and Grayson. The Ellett family was large. U. D. Ellett owned a general merchandise store at Owen's Cross Roads and was very prominent in the community, as well as the church. He was very spiritually minded. He not only subscribed to the *Gospel Advocate*; but also the *Firm Foundation* of Austin, Texas. Alvie H. Ellett, U. D.'s cousin, came to Owen's Cross Roads in 1904 and became postmaster from 1904 until 1906.[200] One can see that the Elletts were influential in this community. The Grayson family was also very prominent. Members of these two families began corresponding with the *Gospel Advocate*, and sometimes the *Firm Foundation*. The first correspondence from one of these families came as a report on a contribution to The McGarvey Orphans' Home And Bible School in Cobb County, Georgia. S. H. Hall commented:

> Brother A. H. Ellett, Owen's Cross Roads, Ala., writes that I may put him and his good wife down for ten dollars. Thank you, Brother Ellett, and we hope to have a school here soon that

will make you and your wife rejoice that you helped to found it.[201]

In July of that year, Ellet and his wife sent money to the Odessa School in Odessa, Missouri in the amount of ten dollars. This demonstrates that the Ellett family supported Christian education.[202]

Moody came back to Owen's Cross Roads for a third mission meeting in August 1909. His meeting continued for thirteen days with no additions.[203]

During this period there apparently was no physician in that community. So, A. H. Ellett (Cousin to "Boss" Ellett) took it upon himself to try and persuade a doctor to move into the Cross Roads area. An advertisement was printed in the *Gospel Advocate* as follows:

> Brother A. H. Ellett, of Owens' Cross Roads. Ala., desires to correspond with a physician with a view to getting him to locate in that community. There is a good opening there to build up a good practice. He is anxious to locate one who is a member of the church of Christ.[204]

As noted, he was hoping for a physician who was a member of the church to come into their vicinity. This shows that Ellett was not only vocal in church affairs, but community affairs. His wife Mable was a strong Christian woman. She had also sent a dollar to the Tennessee Orphans Home.[205] She also sent a dollar to the work for a local congregation in Florida. A dollar, in those days, was a good amount of money. It, along with fifty cents more could buy an acre of land, in certain parts of Alabama and Tennessee.[206]

Moody must have been proud that some of his converts were so caught up in the work of the Lord. He came back in 1911 and held a meeting at Owen's Cross Roads. He still considered this preaching point as mission work. He wrote:

> My next meeting was at Owen's Cross Roads, in Alabama. The meeting continued for ten days and resulted in one addition from the Baptists. This is a mission point and is considered a " hard place." This was the fourth meeting I have held there; and, while the immediate results were meager, the brethren think that more good was done than at any previous meeting. The attendance was good, and the prejudice is giving away. R. N. Moody. [207]

As can be seen, this community was still a difficult place in which to preach the gospel. He referred to it as "a hard place." This, perhaps, was the reason he called it a mission point. He pointed out that this was his fourth meeting there. This tells us that Moody was optimistic for Owen's Cross Roads.

Another family begins to be heard in the *Gospel Advocate*. That was the family of brother C. A. Grayson. He was also perceived as a leader in the church at the Cross Roads. He, like Ellett, was concerned about the spiritual growth in the congregation there. The first member of his family to speak up was his four-year-old son, Charles Albert Grayson, Jr. He inquired about T. B. Larimore's wife Emma, who wrote the Children's Corner in the *Gospel Advocate*. He wanted to tell her that his "Muvver" read the Children's Corner to him and that she also gave him a "Red Letter" edition of the New Testament.[208] Charles Albert's father C. A. Grayson, wrote inquiring about the "holiness movement." His inquiry to Lipscomb was:

> Brother Lipscomb: Please explain in full Mark 16: 17, 18 as there is some excitement among the people as to the meaning of these verses. The "Holiness" people are in our community holding protracted meetings and are claiming that they can pick up serpents and they will not bite them and can drink deadly poison and it will not hurt them; in fact, they have picked up poisonous snakes. They have already taken about ten of our members. Owen's Cross Roads, Ala. C. A. Grayson.[209]

Lipscomb gave a rather lengthy answer to Grayson. The next member of the Grayson family to appear in the *Gospel Advocate* was C. A.'s. wife. She had sent money to Atlanta, Georgia to aid in the work in that city and was named in the contributors' list.[210] One more report, even though it dates beyond our imposed cutoff date (1914) for the work in this book, came in 1919, from J. J. Horton. He gives a close view of the early work at Owen's Cross Roads. His report gave an insight into several local congregations. The account on Owen's Cross Roads stated the following:

> I began my last meeting at Owens Cross Roads, Ala., on the third Lord's day in September. It was such a busy time that 1 preached only at night during the week. The meeting continued for eight days, with thirteen baptisms and one restored to fellowship. I bespeak for these bands of worshipers a very useful career in the Master's vineyard. J. J. Horton.[211]

This draws to a close the sketch relating to Owen's Cross Roads area. Some of the outlying churches in this area disappeared from the pages of recorded history and others either merged with other congregations or perhaps changed their names.

East Huntsville

The next important work to be established, during this time frame, takes us all the way back to Huntsville. This was East Huntsville, sometimes called Dallas Mills in the early days. The earliest glimpse of the work at the Dallas Mills was provided by J. L. Hucks. He wrote of his co-labors with J. D. Jones. The report states:

> Aug. 1: Brother J. D. Jones and the writer began a series of meetings at Dallas Mills the third Lord's day in July, and continued until Friday night, which resulted in one confession and baptism. Notwithstanding the high opposition, we had good hearing all the time. From there we went to Hurricane Grove, my home congregation, where we began preaching on the fourth Lord's day, and continued until Thursday night, which resulted in two confessions and baptisms, and five restored to the faith. Brother Jones is a true gospel preacher, and any church wishing a meeting can write him at 815 Whiteside Street, Chattanooga. I can hold a few more meetings this fall. Any wanting a meeting can write to me in West Huntsville. J. L. Hucks.[212]

East Huntsville was only about ten or eleven miles across the country from Maysville. Hurricane Grove was only four or five miles north of modern-day Maysville. So, it was an easy trip from Dallas Mills to Hurricane Grove, which was Hucks' home. This report is the first mention, in the *Gospel Advocate*, of any efforts to establish a church near the Dallas Mills. At this time, the work was not established; but rather in the first stage of laying the groundwork for the future establishment.

Nine years later W. J. Cullum came and held a meeting at Dallas Mills and found only three or four members. His report is given in full context:

> Nashville, July 24. On the first Lord's day in this month, I began a meeting at Dallas (East Huntsville), Ala., and closed last night. To say the least, the meeting was good all the way through. There was only a small band at work for the Master at the beginning-three or four brethren and about as many sisters; but by having their cooperation in the good work, I believe that much good was accomplished for the Master. The meeting continued for three weeks, with preaching only at night and on Lord's day. The work was under a tent, and it was filled to overflowing at every service during the last two weeks. The result of the work was thirty-eight additions-twenty-five by confessions and baptism and thirteen by reclamation. Among those that were baptized were a number of the sects-Methodists, Baptists, and Presbyterians. Some had been immersed; but all made a good confession and were baptized "unto the remission of sins" according to divine authority. None of them claimed to be satisfied with their baptism; and brethren do you not think that if we would all be as careful along this line of teaching, as we should be, there would be less satisfaction among them about this matter. W. J. Cullum.[213]

A week later W. F. Fulgham drafted a report in which he mentions two interesting facts. He said that "about forty accessions" were gained during Cullum's meeting and that C. Petty was preaching for the congregation at Dallas.[214] That leads one to believe that after Cullum got the work established and left it on good footing; then Petty became their "located" minister.

Cullum returned the following year and conducted another tent meeting. Cullum was from Nashville and supported himself by working for the Timothy Dry Goods Company in Nashville.[215]

He wrote of this meeting also, and described it in detail:

> I have just closed a meeting at Dallas Mills, Huntsville, Ala. The meeting was of fifteen days' duration, and was, I believe, in every way a success. The interest was exceedingly good from the beginning. We had seats for about two hundred and fifty people, but these were sometimes filled by the ladies who came night after night throughout the meeting. The meeting was held under a tent; and owing to the rain, many were kept away. The sects commenced a so-called " union meeting," which proved to be a failure, and after five nights they closed. Eighteen persons were baptized for the remission of sins and into the " one body." Among them were four from the Methodists, three from the Baptists, one from the Presbyterians, and one lady from the Lutheran Church who had received only immersion as they practice it, but who, upon viewing the matter in the true light, was convinced that she had not obeyed the Lord as commanded. Some brother had failed to teach her "the way of the Lord more perfectly," agreeing that she was all right and a member of the one body, in which condition she lived for seventeen years. I am afraid for some brethren who are so careless along this line.[216] I will begin a mission meeting at once for the church on Highland avenue, this city. May the Lord bless all the faithful ones. W. J. Cullum.[217]

Cullum gives a final summation of his summer's work and includes the East Huntsville tent meeting. In this report on his summer's work, he gave a second report on that meeting, he gave no new information relating to the East Huntsville church. This is because he was simply re-capping the entire summer's efforts—which included East Huntsville.[218]

About a month and a half later L. T. Welch, of West Huntsville, gave a very short report on the East and West Huntsville congregations. He said that both congregations were in a "prospering" condition. He also said, "The brethren at Dallas Mills [East Huntsville] are making an effort to build a house in which to worship."[219] In March of 1907 J. P. Watson, of Double Springs, Tennessee, came to Huntsville and held a two-week meeting at Dallas Mills. The *Gospel Advocate* reported the following:

> Brother J. P. Watson, of Double Springs, Tenn., makes the following report of work done: " Beginning on the second Lord' day in March, I preached two weeks at Dallas Mills, Huntsville, Ala., resulting in three baptisms.[220]

At the end of March, a brother Thomas Quillen of Dallas Mills wrote Lipscomb asking three questions:

> Brother Lipscomb: (1) What do you think about foot washing? Is it good or not? (2) What about the holy kiss? (3) What about wearing gold? Dallas Mills, Ala. Thomas Quillen.[221]

Lipscomb answered in his typical "straight to the point" answers. The questions revealed that this struggling new congregation had some issues to work through. This could be called trying to grow spiritually. What we do not know is what was behind these questions. Did Watson cause these questions because of something he might have said in one of his sermons, or did his lessons encourage Quillen to study more and he developed the inquiries as he studied further?

In September 1907, Watson came back and held a second tent meeting at East Huntsville which began on the second Lord's Day and continued until the fifth Lord's Day of September. By September 20 Watson was having "large audiences and good interest" in the tent meeting at Dallas Mills, as reported in the *Gospel Advocate*.[222] Two young men were baptized during this meeting. W. F. Corum wrote:

> Brother Watson sowed the seed of the kingdom, and the blessed Master only knows the good that was done. We all learned to love Brother Watson while he was with us. W. F. Corum.[223]

The next report on the Dallas Mills work was three years later. Brother John Hayes, a native of Limestone County, Alabama, came to Huntsville from Texas and visited his sick brother. While in Huntsville he preached for two weeks in a meeting. Just where the meeting was held is not stated in the report, but he came back to hold several meetings at Dallas Mills. Therefore, we draw the conclusion that this meeting must have been held at Dallas Mills—East Huntsville. Hayes wrote of the meeting:

> Brother John Hayes writes from Huntsville, Ala., under date of March 16: "While in this city at the bedside of my sick child, I have been preaching every night. This is the second week of the meeting, and the interest has been good from the first. On Sunday night many were turned away. We will continue over next Sunday. I expect to return to Texas next week."[224]

In April of 1911 R. N. Moody came and held a meeting of two weeks' length. He wrote:

> My first meeting in 1911 was with the Dallas Mills congregation, Huntsville, Ala. The meeting began on the fourth Sunday in April and continued for two weeks. The attendance and interest were good throughout the meeting, but there were no additions. The congregation here has a new, commodious house, well

seated, well located, and the church seems to be alive to work. R. N. Moody.[225]

This is the first mention of a completed meeting house at East Huntsville. Other than the mention of a completed house of worship, this report gives no further information concerning the work at Dallas Mills. It is interesting that Moody had no visible response. That was not typical for a Moody meeting.

Hayes returned to the Dallas Mills in 1912 for another meeting and the *Gospel Advocate* gave this report:

> Brother. John Hayes writes from Huntsville, Ala., as follows: "I began a meeting last Lord's day with the church of Christ at Dallas Mills; two confessions to elate (June 7), good audience every service, and splendid interest. The meeting is announced over the third Lord's day, and longer if necessary. The Gospel Advocate is 'brimful' of good things these days."[226]

By July 4, Hayes reported that the results were "Thirteen baptisms, two restorations, and two by relation."[227] Hayes' report was followed by a report by John T. Smithson:

> Brother John Hayes conducted a meeting at Dallas Mills. Huntsville, Ala. This meeting continued for two weeks and closed with fifteen people added to the one body. Thirteen of these were baptized, the others were restored and took membership. The meeting, from the human view point, was successful, for there were visible results, yet eternity alone can tell the real good done. Brother Hayes preaches the gospel with force. Anyone who wants to hear the gospel will not be disappointed when they go to hear him. The meeting was well attended. The church arranged for Brother Hayes to conduct another meeting for them next year. After a short visit to his father, at Mooresville, Brother Hayes will go to his home, Cedar Hill, Texas.[228]

Hayes came back to Huntsville in September and preached and had three baptisms and one restoration at East Huntsville and at Merrimac, as of October 3, had one baptism and three restorations.[229] This was Hayes' last trip to Huntsville until 1914.

About four months later Jarrett L. Smith came on a short preaching trip to Huntsville. He came on the first Lord's Day in January (5th of January) and preached at each of the three congregations in Huntsville—East Huntsville, West Huntsville, and finally Randolph Street.[230]

Hayes held the last meeting mentioned in the *Gospel Advocate* before the end of 1914 and reported that the meeting closed with two restored to the fellowship. He wrote—"We thought this meeting a failure, but the brethren say it is one of the best we have held for them."[231] This closes the establishment and early period of the Dallas-East Huntsville work.

West Huntsville

In 1892 a suburban mill was completed and put into operation about two miles west of Huntsville. The West Huntsville Cotton Mills, also steam-powered, had 5,200 spindles. This drew a lot of workers from different parts of north Alabama and southern Tennessee. It was to this mill village that workers came who had been affiliated with the church of Christ in one way or another. That is what drew the first evangelists to this village the following year.

Under the heading —"Churches Planted During the Year." J. D. Gunn is given credit for establishing the West Huntsville congregation. This was in the West Huntsville Cotton Mills district.[232] The month the work began was August 1893. Brother Gunn gave the following report:

> Bell Factory, August 13. Brother J. D. Jones and I closed a meeting at Stevenson, Ala., on Saturday night, July 15th. No additions, but a good interest. On Lord's day I preached at Cedar Grove, about two miles from Stevenson, which resulted in one reclaimed and one from the Adventists. I preached in the Advent church house. The brethren at that place promised to meet on the Lord's day and worship God in his appointed ways.

> From Cedar Grove I went to West Huntsville, Ala., and held a meeting resulting in two baptisms and two reclaimed. Brother J.D. Jones and I closed a meeting at Hurricane, August 6th, which resulted in nine baptisms. Brother E. S. (L.) Cambron and I closed a meeting at Union Grove to-day, which resulted in ten baptisms and two putting away the unscriptural name of Baptist and taking upon them the scriptural name of Christian. If the Lord wills Brother Cambron and I will begin a meeting at Winchester, Tenn., on the third Saturday in August. J.D. Gunn. [233]

This report covered several congregations scattered throughout Madison and Jackson Counties. We also learn that Gunn collaborated with other preachers establishing and strengthening churches.

The following month J. L. Hucks preached at West Huntsville and baptized two young ladies into Christ "the same hour of the night."[234]

The next news about West Huntsville came about three years later. C. Petty moved from Belfast, Tennessee to West Huntsville. He remained through the winter until spring.[235]

S. H. Hall came to Huntsville upon an invitation from brother L. T. Welch to come and preach in a meeting for the straggling band at West Huntsville. In S. H. Hall's autobiography, he gave a graphic picture as to how West Huntsville was organized:

> It was about 1903 [the year was 1904] when Brother Lon Welch, who formerly lived at Gurley, Alabama, asked me to conduct a mission meeting under a tent at West Huntsville, Alabama. There was only one congregation in Huntsville at the time, and the congregation had been in trouble over Brother Daniel Sommer's "Evangelistic Authority" and "Anti-Bible College Ideas." Sommer had been there, the doors locked against him, and he broke in, which precipitated a lawsuit. It was during his trial that our meeting had its beginning, and Brother Sommer

attended one or two of our services — my first time to meet him. Because of the trouble in the up-town congregation, I agreed to conduct the meeting with the distinct understanding that the congregation up-town was to have nothing to do with it. I knew nothing about the merits of their trouble and wanted neither side to have any controlling influence in our meeting, but let it be understood that members from both sides of the fuss would be treated respectfully if they attended, yet none of them was to be used in our services. Enough said about the circumstances under which I went to Huntsville, Alabama.

The slogan that I used quite often in my revivals was — *"God Has Made Himself So Plain and Understandable in All He Has Said to Us About How To Be Saved that Any Two Honest Souls Can See It Exactly Alike."* This slogan was publicized on streamers stretched across the street and on cards placed in much visited places. Everybody was invited to attend and to ask any Bible question that they wished to hear discussed and to offer any criticism about anything that was taught in that meeting, with the assurance that their questions and criticisms would receive polite and courteous attention.[236]

This meeting in June 1904 was not to establish the work but to organize it with elders and deacons. They at once rented a hall and met regularly on the first day of the week for worship.

Ira Jones wrote a short history of the early period of the congregation's history. It was published in S. H. Hall's *Sixty-five Years In The Pulpit.* Jones wrote:

> We started a building fund which resulted in a house of worship the third year. Brother Hall supervised the work for us. He drew up the deed and greatly helped us with the building fund. He assisted in the selection of elders. Brother Hall had the future welfare of the church at heart. He visited the church frequently on the Lord's Day, and we only paid his railroad fare. While he was teaching in the Nashville Bible School, he came often to

help us. One night, after he had gone to his bedroom to retire, I gave him his railroad fare and he said, "Brother Jones, I have four ($4.00) dollars which the brethren handed me, and I want to give it back so that it may be applied on the building and tell the brethren to contribute to the treasury the amount that they want the preacher to have in order that the church may know what is paid to him." The West Huntsville Church loves Brother Hall, not only for his great ability as a preacher, but for his work's sake and the sacrifice he made in helping us in a time of need. Brother Hall conducted three.[237]

Following the tent meeting by Hall, the first mention of the West Huntsville work in the *Gospel Advocate* was sent by L. T. Welch in August 1904. This was the first report after Hall organized the congregation. As this is the earliest report on this work, after organization, we give the full report:

Huntsville, August 22. On the fourth Lord's day in June, Brother S. H. Hall began a tent meeting with the brethren in West Huntsville, which resulted in sixteen additions-twelve by confession and baptism and four by reclamation. The brethren have secured the Odd Fellows' Hall in which to hold their meetings, and the congregation is growing at every service. We want a tent in which to hold a meeting this fall and would be glad if some congregation that has one would let us know about getting it. L. T. Welch.[238]

Hall preached in a tent meeting before the little scattered band in West Huntsville even had a temporary place in which to gather. The tent meeting was the solution for them at the time. This meeting held by Hall in June was followed by another meeting five months later.

The *Gospel Advocate* published a notification that John E. Dunn intended to hold a meeting at West Huntsville in November 1904.[239] He came and began his meeting early in

November and continued until the 20th of that month. Someone reported on Dunn's meeting as follows:

> Brother John E. Dunn writes from West Huntsville, Ala., under date of November 24: Our meeting in West Huntsville closed last Sunday night, with fine interest. We had a fine meeting. My work has been exceptionally encouraging of late.[240]

From this report, we gather that the congregation had no certain meeting place. No tent meeting, no borrowed house. Just where did this meeting take place?

S. H. Hall returned in June of 1905 and held another tent meeting with sixteen additions.[241] We do not know where the tent was placed. By December they were meeting in a vacant warehouse in the cotton mill district in West Huntsville, Alabama.[242] The only mills in that part of Huntsville were the old West Huntsville Cotton Mills and the Merrimack Mills. The congregation was planning to build soon. This group that formed the West Huntsville church is not to be confused with the Merrimac (sometimes spelled Merrimack) church which was a different congregation. Hall closed that meeting with sixteen additions.[243]

The following September (1906) L. T. Welch, of West Huntsville, Alabama, made a visit to the office of the *Gospel Advocate*. He reported the congregations at both West Huntsville and Dallas Mills (East Huntsville) were prospering. He said the brethren at Dallas Mills were trying to build a house in which to worship.[244] He mentioned nothing about a house of worship at the Merrimac Mills.

W. J. Cullum came to Huntsville and labored with both East and West congregations. He reported to the *Gospel Advocate* on these two works:

> Nashville, September 12. I have just returned from my vacation, and as I have reported only one of my meetings, I will now give a brief account of the work I did while away. My first work was

with the brethren at Dallas Mills, Huntsville, Ala. This meeting was held under a tent, as the brethren there have no house of worship. As a result of this work, eighteen people were added to the one body; nine of them were from sectarian organizations. My next meeting was in this city. This was also a tent meeting, supported by the church at Highland avenue. There were two additions by obedience to the gospel, and one was reclaimed during this meeting. Two of them were Methodists.[245]

Both congregations were holding their meetings under tents which suggests that neither congregation had a meeting house of their own. Cullum came back in June 1907 and conducted a series of meetings at West Huntsville.[246] Flavil Hall held a meeting in October 1907.[247] We do not know the results.

Brother J. D. Jones changes his address from Athens, Ala., to Ward Avenue, Huntsville, Ala.[248] He would shortly be engaged in a debate with W. S. Erwin at West Huntsville. Alabama, beginning on the evening of March 2. The report was as follows:

> The propositions to be discussed are: (l) The church with which I am identified is scriptural in doctrine and practice (2) Baptism to a proper subject is for (in order to) the remission of past or alien sins; (3) The Holy Spirit operates in conviction, conversion, and salvation independently or the written or preached word; (4) A child of God may so apostatize as to be finally lost W. S. Erwin affirms the first and third propositions. and J. D. Jones affirms the second and fourth propositions. The brethren at West Huntsville and Merrimac will entertain all those who attend from a distance. If you intend to attend the discussion, write to Brother J. A. Jenkins. West Huntsville, Ala., so that he can supply a home for you.[249]

The result of the Jones-Erwin debate at Merrimac Mills, Huntsville, was one person baptized on the fourth Lord's Day in March.[250]

On the first Lord's Day in April, brother J. D. Jones preached three times at West Huntsville. Ala., and baptized a man and his wife.[251]

S. H. Hall returned for another meeting in April 1908, with the West Huntsville congregation which was reported on the same page of the *Gospel Advocate*.[252]

J. D. Tant held a meeting in Huntsville during June, but it was never specified which part of Huntsville the meeting was held. Tant reported that "twenty-nine persons baptized and three restored to the fellowship."[253] Since it was a tent meeting it could have been one of three locations—West Huntsville, East Huntsville, or Merrimac Mills (at this time still an unorganized band of struggling Christians) since Randolph Street church had their own building. While in Huntsville, Tant was getting brethren to subscribe to the *Firm Foundation*—published by Austin McGary in Austin, Texas. Tant requested of the *Firm Foundation*: "Mail me twenty copys of the *Firm Foundation* there and I will try to send you a club." J. D. Tant.[254]

The fact that Merrimac was unorganized and not counted as a congregation is borne out in a report written by John T. Poe, on June 23, 1909.

> My meeting at this place opens with flattering prospects. We hope for a glorious meeting. There are three churches of Christ here. Two of them East and West Huntsville —doing well.[255]

John A. Jenkins reported John T. Poe's meeting, through the pages of the *Gospel Advocate*. In this report, Jenkins described the congregation's condition:

> West Huntsville, May 26.-The church at this place is progressing nicely. On the third Lord's day in this month Brother Glaze, from Athens, was with us, and preached for us at eleven o'clock; and Brother D. L. Cooper, from Nashville, Tenn., was with us that night, and made us a very instructive talk, and one erring

brother confessed his fault and promised to live better. There was also one erring brother to confess his faults on the fourth Lord's day at our regular Lord's-day service. Brother John T. Poe is expected to begin a meeting here on the third Lord's day in June. We are trying hard to get ready for a good meeting. J. A. Jenkins.[256]

John T. Poe had come to Huntsville for a meeting with the West Huntsville church. His report read:

Brother John T. Poe writes from Huntsville, Ala., under date of June 23: "My meeting at this place opens with flattering prospects. We hope for a glorious meeting. There are three churches of Christ here. Two of them East and West Huntsville —doing well."[257]

His next report on this meeting read:

Brother John T. Poe made this office several pleasant visits during last week. On Monday, July 5, he closed a two-weeks' meeting at West Huntsville, Ala., with four baptized and one restored...[258]

He made one last report in August on this meeting in which he told of boarding with the L. T. Welch family while holding the West Huntsville meeting. He wrote—"I trust they are keeping up the forward move they took on during that meeting."[259]

Some of the brethren had begun subscribing to the Texas paper—the *Firm Foundation*, because of Tant's effort in Huntsville. This was probably the reason another Texas preacher was requested to come to West Huntsville, Alabama.

Two meetings were held during 1910. The first was conducted by W. J. Cullum in May.[260] The second meeting was conducted on November 6, by J. J. Horton, which lasted only one day—resulting in three additions. John A. Jenkins made this report.[261]

In 1911 S. H. Hall returned to West Huntsville and conducted another meeting with eleven baptisms and one restoration.[262] The brethren loved S. H. Hall and contributed monthly to his mission work in Atlanta.[263]

In 1913 J. J. Horton returned and conducted a meeting that lasted "over three Lord's days." John A. Jenkins wrote:

> Huntsville, Ala., June 14.-Brother J. J. Horton, of Elora, Tenn., began a series of meetings here on May 25 and continued over three Lord's days. There were thirteen additions to the congregation-nine by confession and baptism and four by confessing their faults. Brother Horton did some excellent preaching in this meeting. It is wonderful how fast a man can learn the truth when he is willing to lay everything else aside. The church here holds Brother Horton in high esteem and think him a fine preacher. J. A. Jenkins.[264]

With this report, we end our discussion of the church at West Huntsville. The next report was made after our projected date of 1914. The church was originally located at 3105 Eighth Avenue, S.W., Huntsville, until 1975, when the congregation relocated to University and Evangel Drive across from The University of Alabama in Huntsville campus. In 2011 they moved to 1519 Old Monrovia Rd, NW, Huntsville. They are now (2024) known as the West Huntsville Church of Christ at Providence Village.

Merrimack Mills—
Huntsville Park

In 1898, despite its early prominence in textile manufacturing, Huntsville had only three mills—Huntsville Cotton Mills, West Huntsville Cotton Mills, and The Dallas Mills—in operation. It was directly through the efforts of Tracy W. Pratt that the fourth and largest textile plant was chosen to be located in Huntsville. At the time, Pratt was the manager of the West Huntsville Cotton Mills. The new plant was the Merrimack Manufacturing Company, later to become the Huntsville Manufacturing Company, with whose history and progress this story is directly concerned.[265]

About two miles beyond Huntsville, along a winding dirt road leading west by way of the one bridge that spanned Pinhook Creek, lay the small suburban community of West Huntsville. Triana Pike passed south through this community and wound toward the town of Triana some ten miles away on the Tennessee River. On the west side of Triana Pike within the community of West Huntsville was a small brick building where a furniture factory operated periodically. About one block behind the furniture factory stood the West Huntsville Cotton Mills and warehouses, one of the few new industries in Huntsville. It was around the furniture factory and the textile plant that the small community of West Huntsville had grown.[266]

In 1907 W. J. Cullum and W. Wrye came to hold a tent meeting in the Merrimack village of Huntsville, Alabama There was such prejudice against the church that they were not allowed to put up their tent in the village. With the help of the West Huntsville congregation, they pitched the tent just outside the village on Triana Pike and held a three-week meeting, which resulted in sixty-three additions and the beginning of the Merrimack congregation. They met from house to house in the beginning. The next year brother Cullum came for another meeting. By this time, they had received permission to meet in the schoolhouse.

The families of George and Dave Thorneberry were charter members of the church and at the present time, forty-eight years later, six are still here; Mrs. George Thorneberry, Ellen Thorneberry Archer, Florence Thorneberry Preston, Mrs. Dave Thorneberry, Bessie Thorneberry Franklin, and Killie Thorneberry Coop. Other early members of the church were: Frank Gattis, J. W. Wilkes, Beecher Martin, Charlie Russell, and members of their families; also, the Grady family. After their organization in the tent, the Church of Christ met for some time in the school building, which was then a dwelling house at 358-60 North Broad Place.[267]

Cullum gave a personal account of that first meeting and sent it to the *Gospel Advocate*:

> On August 11 Brother W. J. Cullum closed a tent meeting at Merrimack Mills, Huntsville, Ala., with sixty-three baptisms and four restored. This congregation meets in the Merrimack Schoolhouse on the first day of every week to worship the Lord. [268]

A week later John A. Jenkins sent a particularly good report on this meeting. He wrote the following:

MEETING AT MERRIMAC(K) MILLS.
BY J. A. JENKINS.

The church of Christ at West Huntsville, Ala., assisted by a few brethren from Dallas Mills, recently held a series of meetings at Merrimac Mills. Brother W. J. Cullum did the preaching, and it was done right. This is stronghold of the Methodists and Baptists; but the word was preached in its simplicity, error was exposed, Satan was routed, and many souls were led to the truth. As results of the meeting, sixty-three persons were baptized, two erring ones confessed their faults and promised to live better, and two took membership. This was the first gospel preaching ever done here, except a few sermons preached by Brother J. D. Jones some three or four years ago. The opposition was great. We could not get a place to put the tent in the village, so we rented a lot just on the outside and went to work. We are sorry the meeting had to close too soon. A number of people have been heard to say that they were sorry they did not obey the gospel while Brother Cullum was here. The Merrimac Manufacturing Company has agreed for the brethren to have the school building to meet in, and they met on last Lord's day, with about fifty persons in attendance. Some did not know that they would get a place to meet, and some met with the congregation at West Huntsville. So, the good work there continues.[269]

Cullum's report agrees with every other article written about this meeting. We find this to be one of the most documented beginnings of any congregation in Madison County.

Brother J. D. Jones began work in a monthly capacity just a little time later. In March he wrote the *Gospel Advocate*:

Brother J. D. Jones, of Ward avenue, Huntsville, Ala., writes: "The Gospel Advocate has been coming to my address for nearly twenty-five years, and I have always considered it. a great power for good. I am now preaching at the following places once a month: West Huntsville, Merrimack, Paint Rock, and Kennamer Cove. I think that am doing all I can for the cause of the Master. I have no leader but Christ and no guide but his word. I am not working under any board, neither do I belong to anything but the church of God. The man who says I am digressive misrepresents me."[270]

Just over two years later the next report came to the *Gospel Advocate*. Brother Will J. Cullum came back to Huntsville and held a meeting for West Huntsville and one for the Merrimack Mills congregation.[271] Two weeks later the following report was printed in the *Gospel Advocate*:

> Brother Will J. Cullum's meeting at Merrimack Mills, Huntsville. Ala., closed on Friday evening, June 24, with sixteen baptized and eight restored. Brother Cullum is now In a meeting at Paint Rock, Ala.[272]

S. H. Hall came in July of 1911 and held a meeting for the Merrimack congregation. His health failed during the meeting, and he had to end his part. He wrote of this:

> My eleven-day meeting with the brethren at Merrimack, near Huntsville, Ala., closed on Tuesday, June 27, with nine baptized, one from the Baptists, and three restored. I was forced to close on account of physical inability to continue longer. Dr. J. J. Horton, of Ellora, Tenn., kindly consented to do the last baptizing for me and to continue the meeting a few evenings longer.[273]

Dr. J. J. Horton was a popular preacher from Elora and was a preaching companion of J. R. Bradley.

A young preacher North Alabama boy would hold the next meeting. He grew up near Mooresville, Alabama. his name was

John Hayes. Hayes soon became a favorite meeting preacher for the Merrimack congregation. On September 26 it was reported that he was engaged in a meeting at Merrimack.[274] On October 3 it was reported that he had preached at Dallas Mills (East Huntsville) and was back at Merrimack Mills. The results at Merrimack were one baptism and three restorations.[275]

Hayes wrote an appeal on behalf of the struggling work at Merrimack following this meeting. It had almost become his passion to help the congregation there. He titled the appeal "Help Merrimack." The appeal read as follows:

> [Brother John Hayes, who has proved to be an incessant worker and has paid special attention to new fields and struggling churches, presents the following deserving appeal for the brethren at Merrimack (sic) Mills, West Huntsville, Ala. We bespeak a ready response. A. B. L.] (Lipscomb).
>
> The writer held a three-weeks' tent meeting with a faithful few at Merrimack Mills, West Huntsville, Ala. From the first to the last our audiences were large and the interest splendid. As visible results, nine were baptized and six restored. Of the number baptized, there were five Baptists and two Methodists (one a steward in the church. Eternity alone will reveal the good done here. The people lent willing ears to the preaching.
>
> Now, brethren and sisters in Christ, listen. Those brethren have to work hard in the cotton mill for a living. Those of you who have never visited such a place know little of a hard life. They raised three hundred dollars toward building a house of worship. Two hundred more is all they need. Now will not you who have a good house to worship in open your hearts to these good, poor people and help them? The mill company has promised to deed them a lot just as soon as the money is in the bank for the house. Brother, sister, I know many appeals are made, but won't you sacrifice again and help this small band? Send money orders to Frank Gattis, Huntsville, Ala., care of Merrimack Mills. The Lord will bless you in return for your

labor of love in helping others. My address for thirty days will be Trenton, Fla.[276]

This showed the passion in Hayes' words and his desire for the new group to succeed. He would return in 1913 and hold another meeting.

Before Hayes returned, however, Dr. J. J. Horton returned and held a meeting in July. E. L. Cambron co-labored in this meeting with Horton and he described the meeting as follows:

> Winchester, Tenn., July 3.-Dr. J. J. Horton and the writer closed a fine meeting in Huntsville, Ala., on the night of June 29. We preached at night only for two weeks, which resulted in twenty-five additions and others were convinced. The brethren were well pleased with the meeting. Dr. Horton did some fine preaching. Brother Martin of Merrimack conducted the singing, Huntsville, and it was well done. These brethren have no house of worship but are going to make an effort to build it soon. They are good people and need help to get them a house to meet in. Success to the Gospel Advocate. E. L. Cambron.[277]

Twenty-five converts made an exceptionally good number to add to the small band at Merrimack. We learn that a singer was also in the making at Merrimack. Success had to be coming soon.

Hayes came at the end of September and began a meeting.[278] While engaged in this meeting he was also involved in a debate with a Methodist preacher. J. D. Jones said the debate was one-sided.[279] Hayes makes another appeal on behalf of the Merrimack work:

> Brother John Hayes, of Cedar Hill, Texas, calls attention to the struggle that the little band at Merrimack Mills, Huntsville, Ala., is making to get a foothold. These people are in a cotton-factory district. They are poor, but zealous. By dint of labor and sacrifice they have secured a lot and have two hundred dollars in the

bank to be used on the house. They deserve encouragement and fellowship. Send your contribution to Frank Gattis, Huntsville, Ala., care of Merrimack Mills.[280]

Four months later, C. Petty gave an overview of the work in Huntsville, which included Merrimack. The report on the Huntsville work is only a tiny glimpse at the church in that place. It was a full report on three works in Huntsville. Petty wrote:

> Huntsville, Ala., March 16.-Yesterday was a fine day here with all the congregations. The weather was ideal. Sam Pittman preached two strong sermons at Randolph Street Church, with fine attention and good crowds. J. D. Jones preached a fine sermon to a good crowd in the new church house at Merrimac, with splendid attention. Brother Jones said he "dedicated" that church, sure enough. The writer was with the East Town congregation, with about the usual crowd but had splendid attention. Taking it all around, the cause of the Master is improving. We want every brother and sister in this town to work and pray for great success here this year; and if we all work together in perfect harmony and go to see every brother or sister who fails to attend services, we will do a great work here. C. Petty.[281]

We learn from a report by Buford Wilkes, that John Hayes preached the first sermon in the building. Was Wilkes wrong about Hayes preaching the first sermon in the new building? Or did Hayes preach the first sermon in the new building and later Jones dedicated the building?[282] Wilkes was a charter member at Merrimack. His memory was a little faulty on some of the dates, which we confirm in the *Gospel Advocate*.

In July Thomas H. Burton and E. L. Cambron held meetings in Huntsville. Cambron was at Merrimack and Burton was at Dallas Mills. Burton wrote:

Decherd, July 1.—The writer preached for the Dallas congregation, at Huntsville, Ala., on June 21, morning, and night, to attentive audiences. The congregation there seems to be at work. The singing was good. On Monday afternoon I joined E. L. Cambron, of Winchester, Tenn., at Merrimack, where he is conducting a meeting. At the services Thursday night one confessed Christ, and another confessed His name at the water on Friday afternoon. The interest is good. Brother Cambron ranks among the best of our field workers. He presents the truth so plain it seemed even a child could understand it. Thomas H. Burton.[283]

Then Cambron makes his own report on Merrimack:

Winchester, July 6.-I began a meeting with the congregation at Merrimack, Huntsville, Ala., on the second Sunday in June and continued it about ten days. There were six baptized, two reclaimed, and two received from the Baptists. The brethren there are doing well. They have a good Lord's day school and are at peace among themselves. They have completed their new house of worship. E. L. Cambron.[284]

Cambron revealed that the house was finished. This occurred between December 1913 when the congregation was still trying to get funds to build it and July when Cambron said the house was completed.

Even though the following paragraph takes the reader years beyond 1914—the cutoff period, we feel compelled to place a footnote on the history of the Merrimack Congregation. In 1953, during the ministry of R. L. Andrews, the congregation erected a handsome brick building at the northeast corner of Park Boulevard and Ivy Street. It was erected on a lot given to the church by the Huntsville Manufacturing Company and housed a beautiful sanctuary and many Sunday school rooms. It was at this time the congregation became the Huntsville Park congregation. Air conditioning was installed in 1955.[285]

This closes the history of the Merrimack work up to 1914. The congregation continued as the Huntsville Park congregation. In recent years, the congregation closed its doors and sold the building. It is no more!

BEREA—GOOCH LANE

Another congregation was organized near the end of the nineteenth century or early twentieth century. It was about four miles north of Madison Station [present-day Madison]. That was a congregation known in its beginning as Berea. It was located about a block south of the intersection of U.S. Highway 72 and Hughes Road in Madison. It actually sat on Gooch Lane where Gooch Lane turned west off Hughes Road.

A possible reference to this Berea was by R. W. Officer who had preached all around the region where Berea was located. He referred to Berea along with Reunion and Oakland, which were just to the west of Berea, and located in Limestone County.[286] If Officer is referring to another Berea—the nearest one was Berea in Marshall County which was seventy-five miles away. If Officer is referring to the Madison County Berea that puts the establishment of the congregation, at least in the 1880's or even earlier. But we have no solid proof of the beginning date.

The first mention of a Berea in Madison County, Alabama [beyond any doubt] is found in the *Gospel Advocate*. This we know refers to the Berea near Madison, which was in 1899. The report stated:

> Brother J. W. Shepherd, of this city, will begin a meeting at Berea, Madison County, Ala., on the third Lord's day in July. [287]

Shepherd had been coming to the Huntsville area quite regularly at this time and was preaching for some new struggling congregations—Berea being one such congregation. We do not know who was responsible for the establishment of this congregation. It could possibly have been Shepherd. We just do not know at this time.

The next report on this new work was published in 1902. It was made by a T. G.:

> Madison Station, August 16. — On the fourth Lord's day in July Brother George C. Waggoner, of Lexington, Ky., began a meeting at Berea, four miles north of this place. The meeting continued for about ten days. The attendance and attention were good, and the meeting resulted in sixteen additions. T.G. [288]

It would be nearly four years before the next report came in 1906. It was reported that L. B. Jones came and preached on January 21, 1906. Jones described the congregation as— "being active and aggressive in the master's work."[289] He came back and held a gospel meeting in August 1906. The results were "six baptisms and one from the Baptists."[290] The meeting lasted one week.

By 1907 L. B. Jones was said to be preaching for Berea. We understand that to mean that Jones was preaching regularly for Berea. In this short report it was revealed that Berea's work was "progressing nicely."[291]

Jones held a successful meeting in July of 1907, beginning on the third Lord's Day in July.[292] Another report was made about this meeting on August 8, 1907. The results were five baptisms. [293]

The next year in July H. C. Shoulders came and held a meeting in the month of July. The report stated:

> Brother H. C. Shoulders made this office a very pleasant visit during last week. He had just closed a good meeting at Bethel, near Greenbrier, Tenn., with six baptisms. He is now in a meeting at Berea, near Madison, Ala.[294]

We know nothing of the results of this meeting. It was never reported in the *Gospel Advocate*. Charles L. Talley conducted the next meeting with five baptisms and one restoration.[295]

In 1911 J. T. Harris of Florence came to Berea and conducted a meeting that was reported in the *Gospel Advocate*:

> Brother J. T. Harris, of Florence, Ala., recently closed an eight-days' meeting at Berea, four miles north of Madison, Ala., with four baptized. He is now in a meeting at Macedonia, near Florence, Ala.[296]

Harris returned and held another meeting in January of 1912. The *Gospel Advocate* reported a short line concerning this meeting but no results were ever reported. Later that year John T. Hines held a meeting and six were baptized—two came from the Baptists and one restored.[297]

Isaac C. Hoskins from Popular Street in Florence, Alabama came and held a meeting from August 24 through August 31 of 1913. He preached fifteen sermons. He reported three baptisms. He wrote of Berea:

> ... splendid audiences. The common mistake of quitting too soon was made, but a "busy season" was at hand. A delightfully hospitable and sociable people constitute the little church at Berea.[298]

This would be the last report within our time limit from the beginning up to 1914.

Nothing could be found in the pages of the *Gospel Advocate* from 1913 until 1926 relating to Berea. From 1926 until 1929 three men's names stand out—W. H. Broughton, Boyd Fanning, and L. B. Jones. These men conducted several meetings at Berea during this period. Through the 1930s and 1940s other men's names came to prominence at Berea. Rufus David Underwood, Homer P. Reeves, and Marshall E. Patton became popular preachers in gospel meetings at Berea. Later Berea built a new house of worship and changed the name to Gooch Lane. Today the new building brought a new name. It is now known as the "Church of Christ Hughes Road at Gooch Lane."

We conclude our study of the Restoration Movement in Madison County, Alabama. We had selected the year World War I began (1914) as our ending period for research and writing a history for the entire state. There may have been other congregations that were established within our set time, but no written material could be found on them if they ever existed; therefore, we have not written about what we cannot verify. Maybe in the future, some researchers may discover some source or sources that will shed more light upon the movement in Madison County, Alabama.

Endnotes

[1] Government Land Office, Washington, D.C., September 18, 1809, Certificate # 473.

[2] Abner Hill, *An Autobiography Of Abner Hill — Pioneer Preacher In Tennessee, Alabama And Texas*, 15–18.

[3] Kate Powell Evans, compiler, *A Collection of Green County History* (Greensburg, KY: Green County Library, 1976).

[4] Terry Cowan, *A Matthews History*, 259.

[5] John August Williams, *Life of Elder John Smith* (Cincinnati, OH: R. W. Carroll & Co., Publishers, 1870), 99.

[6] Williams, *Life of Elder John Smith*, 99.

[7] Williams, *Life of Elder John Smith*, 101.

[8] Williams, *Life of Elder John Smith*, 101

[9] Williams, *Life of Elder John Smith*, 462–63.

[10] Donald Alfred Nunnelly, "The Disciples of Christ in Alabama, 1860-1910," (The College of the Bible, Lexington, KY, 1954).

[11] B. F. Hall, *Autobiography*, 30.

[12] *Gospel Advocate* (November 19, 1884), 743.

[13] *Gospel Advocate* (May 16, 1946), 472.

[14] *Gospel Advocate* (May 12, 1966), 301.

[15] B. F. Hall, *Autobiography*, 30.

[16] B. F. Hall, *Autobiography*, 30–31.

[17] *The Huntsville Historical Review* (Published By The Huntsville-Madison County Historical Society, 2008, 128.

[18] *The [Huntsville] Democrat*, on July 29, 1825.

[19] *Christian Messenger* (October 25, 1827), 227.

[20] *Gospel Advocate* (August 27, 1874), 805–06.

[21] *Millennial Harbinger* (June 1859), 356–57.

[22] *Christian Review* (June 1845), 144.

[23] *Christian Review* (September 1845), 255–56.

[24] (Index to the Executive Documents of the 27th Congress, 2nd session —1841–42, 195).

[25] *Millennial Harbinger* (April 1834), 192.

[26] *Evangelist* (June 2, 1834), 132–33.

[27] *Christian Messenger* (October 1834), 318.

[28] *Christian Review* (November 1844), 243.

[29] *Gospel Advocate* (January 26, 1882), 55.

[30] *Christian Review* (February 1844), 47.

[31] *Christian Review* (August 1844), 192.

[32] *Christian Review* (September 1844), 215.

[33] *Christian Review* (November 1844), 243.

[34] *Christian Review* (August 1845), 192.

[35] *Millennial Harbinger* (November 1845), 527.

[36] George H. Watson, and Mildred B. Watson, *The Christian Churches In The Alabama Area* (St. Louis, MO: The Bethany Press, 1965).

[37] Asa Plyler, *Churches of Christ in Alabama* (Henderson, TN: Hester Publications, n.d.), 34.

[38] F. D. Srygley, *Seventy Years In Dixie* (Nashville, TN: Gospel Advocate Publishing, 1891), 359.

[39] *Gospel Advocate* (August 10, 1876), 743.

[40] *Gospel Advocate* (November 20, 1879), 745.

[41] *Gospel Advocate* (September 16, 1880), 604.

[42] *Gospel Advocate* (April 30, 1884), 283.

[43] U.S. Hayes Store, District 1, Madison County 1860, p. 2.

[44] *Gospel Advocate* (September 8, 1881), 566.

[45] *Gospel Advocate* (July 6, 1882), 427.
[46] *Gospel Advocate* (November 11, 1880, 728.
[47] F. D. Srygley, *Smiles and Tears: or Larimore and His Boys* (Nashville, TN: Gospel Advocate Company, 1898), 198.
[48] *Gospel Advocate* (February 24, 1881), 121.
[49] *Gospel Advocate* (February 24, 1881), 121.
[50] *Gospel Advocate* (March 3, 1881), 139.
[51] *Gospel Advocate* (April 14, 1881), 235.
[52] *Gospel Advocate* (April 28, 1881), 267.
[53] *Gospel Advocate* (May 5, 1881), 283.
[54] *Gospel Advocate* (August 17, 1882), 523.
[55] *Gospel Advocate* (December 7, 1882), 775.
[56] *Gospel Advocate* (December 21, 1882), 806.
[57] *Gospel Advocate* (January 11, 1883), 19.
[58] *Gospel Advocate* (March 15, 1883), 161.
[59] *Gospel Advocate* (January 18, 1883), 41.
[60] *Gospel Advocate* (February 8, 1883), 84.
[61] *Gospel Advocate* (February 8, 1883), p. 84.
[62] *Gospel Advocate* (April 30. 1884), 283.
[63] *Firm Foundation* (July 25, 1889), 6.
[64] *Gospel Advocate* (August 8, 1907), 501.
[65] *Gospel Advocate* (August 14, 1913), 781.
[66] Srygley, *Smiles and Tears,* 198–99.
[67] *Gospel Advocate* (July 7, 1886), 427.
[68] *Gospel Advocate* (February 10, 1881), 87.
[69] *Gospel Advocate* (July 5, 1877), 422.
[70] *Gospel Advocate* (April 18, 1883), 251.
[71] *Gospel Advocate* (May 23, 1883), 331.
[72] *Gospel Advocate* (May 9, 1883), 299.
[73] *Gospel Advocate* (May 16, 1883), 315.
[74] *Gospel Advocate* (March 19, 1884), 184.
[75] *Gospel Advocate* (October 1, 1884), 631.
[76] *Gospel Advocate* (March 19, 1884), 170.
[77] *Gospel Advocate* (October 1, 1884), 631.
[78] *Gospel Advocate* (October 1, 1884), 631.

[79] *Gospel Advocate* (March 11, 1885), 150.
[80] *Gospel Advocate* (March 11, 1885), 151.
[81] *Gospel Advocate* (March 11, 1885), 151.
[82] *Gospel Advocate* (March 18, 1885), 167.
[83] *Gospel Advocate* (March 25, 1885), 186.
[84] *Gospel Advocate* (February 8, 1888), 8-9.
[85] *Gospel Advocate* (April 30. 1884), 283.
[86] *Gospel Advocate* (June 3, 1885), 343.
[87] *Gospel Advocate* (March 3, 1886), 135.
[88] *Gospel Advocate* (March 10, 1886), 152.
[89] *Gospel Advocate* (April 1, 1885), 202.
[90] *Gospel Advocate* (April 1, 1885), 202.
[91] *Gospel Advocate* (March 3, 1886), 135.
[92] *Gospel Advocate* (March 10, 1886), 152.
[93] *Gospel Advocate* (June 2, 1886), 343.
[94] *Gospel Advocate* (June 2, 1886), 343.
[95] *Gospel Advocate* (January 18, 1883), 41.
[96] *Gospel Advocate* (June 23, 1886), 399.
[97] *Gospel Advocate* (June 23, 1886), 399.
[98] *Gospel Advocate* (July 7, 1886), 427.
[99] *Gospel Advocate* (July 7, 1886), 427.
[100] *Gospel Advocate* (June 3, 1885), 343.
[101] *Gospel Advocate* (June 30, 1886), 414.
[102] *Huntsville Mercury* (Huntsville, AL).
[103] Gospel Advocate (December 1, 1886), 762.
[104] *Gospel Advocate* (January 12, 1887), 30.
[105] *Gospel Advocate* (June 22, 1887), 385.
[106] *Gospel Advocate* (November 27, 1889), 762.
[107] *Gospel Advocate* (December 18, 1889), 811.
[108] *Gospel Advocate* (December 25, 1889), 826.
[109] *Gospel Advocate* (December 25, 1889), 826.
[110] *Gospel Advocate* (January 1, 1890), 10.
[111] *Gospel Advocate* (May 19, 1892), 316.
[112] *Gospel Advocate* (June 2, 1892), 341.
[113] *Gospel Advocate* (June 9. 1892), 364.

[114] *Gospel Advocate* (June 9. 1892), 364.
[115] *Gospel Advocate* (December 20), 1894, 795.
[116] *Gospel Advocate* (July 25, 1895), 477.
[117] *Gospel Advocate* (April 20, 1898), 245.
[118] *Gospel Advocate* (September 9, 1897), 561.
[119] *Gospel Advocate* (September 9, 1897), 561.
[120] *Gospel Advocate* (September 9, 1897), 561.
[121] *Gospel Advocate* (September 9, 1897), 562.
[122] *Gospel Advocate* (October 28, 1897, 673.
[123] *Gospel Advocate* (February 10, 1898, 92.
[124] *Gospel Advocate* (February 10, 1898), 92.
[125] *Gospel Advocate* (January 19, 1899), 37.
[126] *Gospel Advocate* (October 26, 1899), 677.
[127] Watson, *History Of The Christian Churches in The Alabama Area*, 199–200.
[128] *Gospel Advocate* (July 19, 1900), 453.
[129] *Gospel Advocate* (April 25, 1901), 269.
[130] *Gospel Advocate* (November 28, 1901), 757.
[131] *Gospel Advocate* (February 27, 1902), 133.
[132] *Gospel Advocate* (April 17, 1902), 245.
[133] *Gospel Advocate* (June 26, 1902), 405.
[134] *Gospel Advocate* (September 18, 1902), 597.
[135] *Gospel Advocate* (October 2, 1902), 637.
[136] *Gospel Advocate* (November 27, 1902), 757.
[137] *Gospel Advocate* (June 30, 1904), 413.
[138] *Gospel Advocate* (July 13, 1905), 443.
[139] *Gospel Advocate* (August 31, 1905), 549.
[140] *Gospel Advocate* (July 6, 1906), 421.
[141] *Gospel Advocate* (January 17, 1907), 41.
[142] *Gospel Advocate* (November 28, 1907), 757.
[143] *Gospel Advocate* (September 16, 1909), 1172.
[144] *Gospel Advocate* (July 13, 1905), 443.
[145] *Gospel Advocate* (February 3, 1916), 118.
[146] Gospel Advocate (December 7, 1911), 1424.
[147] *Gospel Advocate* (February 1, 1912), 156.

[148] *Gospel Advocate* (June 20, 1912), 740.
[149] *Gospel Advocate* (August 15, 1912), 914.
[150] *Gospel Advocate* (March 20, 1913), 283.
[151] *Gospel Advocate* (January 16, 1913), 60.
[152] *Gospel Advocate* (February 20, 1913), 180.
[153] *Gospel Advocate* (March 27, 1913), 301.
[154] *Gospel Advocate* (May 22, 1913), 493.
[155] *Gospel Advocate* (June 5, 1913), 540.
[156] *Gospel Advocate* (July 10, 1913), 660.
[157] *Gospel Advocate* (January 8, 1914), 50.
[158] *Gospel Advocate* (March 20, 1913), 283.
[159] *Gospel Advocate* (April 2, 1914), 376.
[160] *Gospel Advocate* (April 23, 1914), 452.
[161] *Gospel Advocate* (November 11, 1880), 728.
[162] *Gospel Advocate* (September 19, 1888), 14.
[163] *Gospel Advocate* (April 10, 1889), 238.
[164] *Gospel Advocate* (July 24, 1889), 474.
[165] *Gospel Advocate* (October 24, 1901), 685.
[166] *Gospel Advocate* (October 11, 1906), 652.
[167] *Gospel Advocate* (August 15, 1907), 517.
[168] *Gospel Advocate* (September 5, 1907), 572.
[169] *Gospel Advocate* (September 24, 1908), 618.
[170] *Gospel Advocate* (November 12, 1908), 735.
[171] *Gospel Advocate* (August 11, 1910), 928.
[172] *Gospel Advocate* (September 29, 1910), 1093.
[173] *Gospel Advocate* (September 14, 1911), 1046.
[174] *Gospel Advocate* (August 29, 1912), 980.
[175] *Gospel Advocate* (May 5, 1927), 425.
[176] *Gospel Advocate* (May 28, 1890), 350.
[177] *Gospel Advocate* (September 9, 1891), 572.
[178] *Gospel Advocate* (August 24, 1893), 533.
[179] *Gospel Advocate* (May 10, 1894), 289.
[180] *Gospel Advocate* (May 5, 1927), 425.
[181] *Gospel Advocate* (June 3, 1897), 344.
[182] *Gospel Advocate* (October 13, 1904), 653.

[183] *Gospel Advocate* (September 11, 1913), 879.
[184] *Gospel Advocate* (May 28, 1890), 350.
[185] *Gospel Advocate* (October 8, 1896), 652.
[186] *Gospel Advocate* (August 23, 1906), 540.
[187] *Gospel Advocate* (October 11, 1906), 652.
[188] *Gospel Advocate* (September 5, 1907), 557.
[189] *Gospel Advocate* (July 10, 1908), 485.
[190] *Gospel Advocate* (August 13, 1908), 517.
[191] *Gospel Advocate* (Sept. 21, 1893), 601.
[192] *Gospel Advocate* (May 9, 1918), 452.
[193] *Gospel Advocate* (October 9, 1924), 981.
[194] *Gospel Advocate* (September 7, 1911), 1008.
[195] *Gospel Advocate* (April 2, 1914), 380.
[196] *Gospel Advocate* (November 11, 1880), 728.
[197] Harold Kelley, Class Paper by Harold Kelley, who personally interviewed family members of 'Boss" Ellett and R. N. Moody.
[198] *Gospel Advocate* (September 12, 1907), 588.
[199] *Gospel Advocate* (November 12, 1908), 735.
[200] Harold Kelley, Class Paper by Harold Kelley, who personally interviewed family members of 'Boss" Ellett and R. N. Moody.
[201] *Gospel Advocate* (February 25, 1909), 255 (31).
[202] *Gospel Advocate* (July 1, 1909), 828.
[203] *Gospel Advocate* (September 16, 1909), 1172.
[204] *Gospel Advocate* (January 27, 1910), 112.
[205] *Gospel Advocate* (March 7, 1912), 312.
[206] *Gospel Advocate* (June 21, 1912), 767.
[207] *Gospel Advocate* (November 2, 1911), 1279.
[208] *Gospel Advocate* (March 16, 1911), 330.
[209] *Gospel Advocate* (September 11, 1913), 875.
[210] *Gospel Advocate* (January 30, 1913), 113.
[211] *Gospel Advocate* (October 16, 1919), 1031.
[212] *Gospel Advocate* (August 13, 1896), 525.
[213] *Gospel Advocate* (August 3, 1905), 493.

[214] *Gospel Advocate* (August 10, 1905), 501.
[215] *Gospel Advocate* (July 12, 1906), 437.
[216] 2 Tim. 3: 5 (KJV).
[217] *Gospel Advocate* (August 2, 1906), 492.
[218] *Gospel Advocate* (September 20, 1906), 604–05.
[219] *Gospel Advocate* (September 20, 1906), 597.
[220] *Gospel Advocate* (June 13, 1907), 373.
[221] *Gospel Advocate* (March 28, 1907), 198.
[222] *Gospel Advocate* (October 10, 1907), 645.
[223] *Gospel Advocate* (November 7, 1907), 716.
[224] *Gospel Advocate* (March 24, 1910), 308.
[225] *Gospel Advocate* (November 2, 1911), 1278.
[226] *Gospel Advocate* (June 13, 1912), 716.
[227] *Gospel Advocate* (July 4, 1912), 788.
[228] *Gospel Advocate* (July 11, 1912), 820.
[229] *Gospel Advocate* (October 3, 1912), 1101.
[230] *Gospel Advocate* (March 20, 1913), 283.
[231] *Gospel Advocate* (September 11, 1913), 878.
[232] *Gospel Advocate* (November 9, 1893), 708.
[233] *Gospel Advocate* (August 24, 1893), p533.
[234] *Gospel Advocate* (September 21, 1893), 601.
[235] *Gospel Advocate* (January 2, 1896), 8.
[236] S. H. Hall, *Sixty-five Years in The Pulpit*, Nashville, TN: Gospel Advocate Company, 1954), 136.
[237] S. H. Hall, *Sixty-five Years in The Pulpit*, 139.
[238] *Gospel Advocate* (September 8, 1904), 572.
[239] *Gospel Advocate* (November 1, 1904), 709.
[240] *Gospel Advocate* (December 1, 1904), 757.
[241] *Gospel Advocate* (June 15, 1905), 373.
[242] *Gospel Advocate* (December 28, 1905), 821.
[243] *Gospel Advocate* (July 13, 1905), 437.
[244] *Gospel Advocate* (September 20, 1906), 597.
[245] *Gospel Advocate* (September 20, 1906), 604—5.
[246] *Gospel Advocate* (June 13, 1907), 373.
[247] *Gospel Advocate* (October 17, 1907), 661.

[248] *Gospel Advocate* (February 6, 1908), 85.
[249] *Gospel Advocate* (February 27, 1908), 133.
[250] *Gospel Advocate* (April 9, 1908), 229.
[251] *Gospel Advocate* (April 23, 1908), 261.
[252] *Gospel Advocate* (April 23, 1908), 261.
[253] *Gospel Advocate* (July 16, 1908), 453.
[254] *Firm Foundation* (January 7, 1908), 2.
[255] *Gospel Advocate* (July 1, 1909), 816.
[256] *Gospel Advocate* (June 3, 1909), 696.
[257] *Gospel Advocate* (July 1, 1909), 816.
[258] *Gospel Advocate* (July 15, 1909), 880.
[259] *Gospel Advocate* (August 19, 1909), 1049.
[260] *Gospel Advocate* (May 26, 1910), 644.
[261] *Gospel Advocate* (November 24. 1910), 1305.
[262] *Gospel Advocate* (June 22, 1911), 684.
[263] *Gospel Advocate* (February 29, 19120, 285.
[264] *Gospel Advocate* (June 19, 1913), 589.
[265] Sarah Huff Fisk, ed., *The Huntsville Parker, Historical Edition*, (Huntsville, AL: Huntsville Manufacturing Company, September 1955), 8.
[266] Fisk, ed., *The Huntsville Parker*, 9.
[267] Fisk, ed., *The Huntsville Parker*, 40.
[268] *Gospel Advocate* (September 5, 1907), 549.
[269] *Gospel Advocate* (September 12, 1907), 591.
[270] *Gospel Advocate* (March 26, 1908), 197.
[271] *Gospel Advocate* (June 16, 1910), 716.
[272] *Gospel Advocate* (June 30, 1910), 764.
[273] *Gospel Advocate* (July 6, 1911), 732.
[274] *Gospel Advocate* (September 26, 1912), 1076.
[275] *Gospel Advocate* (October 3, 1912), 1101.
[276] *Gospel Advocate* (October 17, 1912), 1157.
[277] *Gospel Advocate* (July 10, 1913), 661.
[278] *Gospel Advocate* (October 2, 1913), 948.
[279] *Gospel Advocate* (October 16, 1913), 996.
[280] *Gospel Advocate* (December 18, 1913), 1247.

[281] *Gospel Advocate* (April 2, 1914), 376.
[282] *Gospel Advocate* (November 28, 1940), 1150.
[283] *Gospel Advocate* (July 16, 1914), 777.
[284] *Gospel Advocate* (July 16, 1914), 777.
[285] Fisk, ed., *The Huntsville Parker*, 40.
[286] *Gospel Advocate* (January 26, 1887), 55.
[287] *Gospel Advocate* (July 13, 1899), 437.
[288] *Gospel Advocate* (August 28, 1902), 556.
[289] *Gospel Advocate* (January 25, 1906), 53.
[290] *Gospel Advocate* (August 16, 1906), 517.
[291] *Gospel Advocate* (February 21, 1907), 117.
[292] *Gospel Advocate* (August 1, 1907), 485.
[293] *Gospel Advocate* (August 8, 1907), 501.
[294] *Gospel Advocate* (July 23, 1908), 469.
[295] *Gospel Advocate* (August 27, 1908), 549.
[296] *Gospel Advocate* (August 24, 1911), 944.
[297] *Gospel Advocate* (September 5, 1912), 1005.
[298] *Gospel Advocate* (September 11, 1913), 876.

Bibliography

Books

John D. Cox, *A Word Fitly Spoken* (Nashville, TN: Gospel Advocate Company, 1963), 22.

Evans, Kate Powell, compiler. *A Collection of Green County History.* Greensburg, KY: Green County Library, 1976.

Sarah Huff Fisk, ed. *The Huntsville Parker, Historical Edition.* Huntsville, AL: Huntsville Manufacturing Company, September 1955.

Hall, S. H. *Sixty-five Years in The Pulpit.* Nashville, TN: Gospel Advocate Company, 1954.

The Huntsville Historical Review. Published By The Huntsville-Madison County Historical Society, 2008.

Nunnelly, Donald Alfred. "The Disciples of Christ in Alabama, 1860-1910." The College of the Bible, Lexington, KY, 1954.

Plyler, Asa. *Churches of Christ in Alabama.* Henderson, TN: Hester Publications, n.d.

Srygley, F. D. *Seventy Years In Dixie.* Nashville, TN: Gospel Advocate Publishing, 1891.

——— *Smiles and Tears: or Larimore and His Boys.* Nashville, TN: Gospel Advocate Company, 1898.

Watson, George H. and Mildred B. Watson. *The Christian Churches In The Alabama Area.* St. Louis, MO: The Bethany Press, 1965.

Williams, John August. *Life of Elder John Smith.* Cincinnati, OH: R. W. Carroll & Co., 1870.

Periodicals

Christian Messenger
Christian Review
Evangelist
Firm Foundation
Gospel Advocate
The [Huntsville] Democrat
Huntsville Mercury
Millennial Harbinger

Name Index

Barnes, Justus McDuffie 53–57, 61, 77
Biard, John Nelson 14
Bradley, J. R. 70, 98, 102, 105–107, 135
Cambron, E. L. 81, 83, 87, 100–102, 124, 137–139
Campbell, Alexander ix, xiv–xv, 7–8, 14–15, 18
Chisholm, John viii, 3–5, 8
Collins, Ira F. 65, 69, 72, 78–81, 83–84
Cullum, W. J. 117–118, 127–128, 130, 133–135
D'Spain, Marshall 3, 5, 8
Dunn, G. A. 90, 96, 99
Dunn, John E. 126–127
Ellett, A. H. 112–114
Ellett, U. D. 95, 110, 112–113, 151
Elley, George W. 22–25
Fanning, Tolbert viii, 15–16, 21–22, 24
Goodwin, B. C. 69–70, 92–94, 101
Gunn, J. D. 101, 123–124

Hall, Benjamin Franklin viii, 10
Hall, S. H. 112, 124–127, 129, 131, 135, 145,– 146, 152
Harding, James A. 37–39, 41, 45–46, 48–49, 56, 63–64, 75
Harris, J. T. 143
Hastings, R. J. 100–102
Hayes, John 120–122, 136–138
Henry, A. C. 51
Hill, Abner 4, 145
Horton, J. J. 42, 102, 115, 131, 135, 137
Hoskins, Isaac C. 143
Hucks, J. L. 116–117, 124
Hundley, John Henry 43–44
Hundley, Orville Marion 40–41, 47, 50, 52, 54, 64, 69
Hundley, Oscar 44, 50, 52
Jenkins, John A. 128–131, 133–134
Jones, J. D. 116, 123–124, 128–129, 134, 137–138

Jones, Luther B.   42, 104–105, 142, 144
Larimore, T. B.   xi, xv, 35, 37, 43–45, 53, 58–59, 64, 66–69, 71–73, 76, 83, 114, 146
Lipscomb, David   38, 40–41, 46–48, 60–61, 65–66, 71, 84, 101–102, 114–115, 119
Lipscomb, Granville   30, 75
Little, T. C.   8, 85, 98
Lynn, Benjamin   viii, xiv–xv, 3–5
Matthews, James E.   viii, 3–4, 14
McMullen, Amanda F.   36–37, 40, 48–50, 52–53, 55–56, 60–61, 64, 73, 83
Metcalfe, V. M.   39–41, 50, 52–53, 56
Moody, R. N.   84–85, 95–999, 110–114, 120–121, 151
Morris, J. H.   92–94
Morris, J. H. of New Hope   32–33, 92, 109–110
Morton, James H.   105
Norwood, R. W.   58–59
Officer, Robert Wallace   30–31, 141
Petty, C.   79, 83, 90–91, 117–118, 124, 138
Pittman, Samuel Parker   89–91, 138
Poe, John T.   129–130
Pullias, C. M.   89, 91
Randolph, C. L.   15
Scott, Walter   19

Shepherd, J. W.   8, 31, 42, 46–49, 142
Smith, F. W.   75, 77, 79–81
Smith, Jarrett L.   88, 90, 122
Smith, John (Raccoon)   5, 7, 20–21
Smithson, John T.   86–91, 121
Spiegel, Oliver Pickens   64–66, 72–73, 75–77
Srygley, F. D.   xi, xv, 28, 35, 37, 43, 65, 75, 146–147
Stone, Barton Warren   xiv, 8, 13–14, 93
Talley, Charles L.   90, 95, 98–99, 107, 143
Tant, J. D.   129–130
Welch, L. T.   119, 124, 126–127, 130
Wilson, L. H.   36–40

Also by C. Wayne Kilpatrick

An Early History of the Mars Hill Church of Christ: With a Collection of Memories by Members of the Congregation (2024)

J. R. Bradley: A Forgotten Larimore Boy (2019)

John Chisholm Church History Series

including

A Little Band of Disciples: The Beginnings of Churches of Christ in Madison County, Alabama

A Faithful Band of Workers: The Beginnings of Churches of Christ in Jackson County, Alabama

A Noble Band of Worshipers: The Beginnings of Churches of Christ Lauderdale County, Alabama

A Small Band of Brethren: The Beginnings of Churches of Christ in Limestone County, Alabama

CYPRESS

To see the full catalog of Heritage Christian University Press and its imprint, Cypress Publications, visit
www.hcupress.edu

www.ingramcontent.com/pod-product-compliance
Lightning Source LLC
Chambersburg PA
CBHW020245010526
44107CB00002B/101